Praise for
America and the Future of War

"While America's leaders display scant understanding of war, Williamson Murray again provides an unflinching book exposing realities we cannot ignore. The breadth and clarity of this richly researched primer packs lens-changing messages on every page, reflecting the author's extraordinary analytic rigor and historical insight. A must-read if we're to escape the morass of nonstrategic thinking endangering our future."

—*General James Mattis, US Marine Corps (ret)*

"This short but wide-ranging book is a like a necessary splash of cold water in the face of the academic and military establishments. There is the drama of a great, take-no-prisoners essay about it. The future of war, the author rightly says, will be like the past: bloody and unpredictable."

—*Robert D. Kaplan, senior fellow, Center for a New American Security and author of* The Coming Anarchy *and* The Revenge of Geography

"A superbly written analysis of how the world that we inhabit could go terribly wrong in the decades ahead. For those who think major wars are now impossible because of the 'democratic peace' or nuclear deterrence, Murray cautions us to look at history and think again. *America and the Future of War* should be mandatory reading for all senior political and military leaders, including those in Congress, the executive branch, and all four military services."

—*Peter Mansoor, colonel, US Army (ret.) General Raymond E. Mason Jr. Chair of Military History Ohio State University*

"Williamson Murray's aim in *America and the Future of War* is twofold: he offers a tragic reminder to often therapeutic- minded Americans that war is inherent in the human condition and cannot be legislated or thought away. But he also offers a second practical blueprint of how the United States, through military readiness, deterrence, a balance of power, and muscular alliances, can prevent or at least mitigate hostile aggression. A tour de force of historical insight and political acumen."

—*Victor Davis Hanson, Martin and Illie Anderson Senior Fellow in Classics and Military History, Hoover Institution*

AMERICA and the
FUTURE of WAR

The Hoover Institution gratefully acknowledges
the following individuals and foundations
for their significant support of the

HERBERT AND JANE DWIGHT WORKING GROUP
ON ISLAMISM AND THE INTERNATIONAL ORDER:

Herbert and Jane Dwight

Donald and Joan Beall
   Beall Family Foundation

S. D. Bechtel, Jr. Foundation

Lynde and Harry Bradley Foundation

Stephen and Susan Brown

Lakeside Foundation

AMERICA and the FUTURE of WAR

The Past as Prologue

WILLIAMSON MURRAY

Ambassador Anthony D. Marshall Professor
Marine Corps University

Professor Emeritus
The Ohio State University

HOOVER INSTITUTION PRESS
STANFORD UNIVERSITY | STANFORD, CALIFORNIA

www.hoover.org

Hoover Institution Press Publication No. 674

Hoover Institution at Leland Stanford Junior University,
Stanford, California, 94305–6003

First printing 2017

23 22 21 20 19 18 17   9 8 7 6 5 4 3 2 1

Manufactured in the United States of America

The paper used in this publication meets the minimum requirements of the American National Standard for Information Sciences—Permanence of Paper for Printed Library Materials, ANSI/NISO Z39.48–1992.

Cataloging-in-Publication Data is available from the Library of Congress.
ISBN 978-0-8179-2004-3 (cloth : alk. paper)
ISBN 978-0-8179-2006-7 (EPUB)
ISBN 978-0-8179-2007-4 (Mobipocket)
ISBN 978-0-8179-2008-1 (PDF)

CONTENTS

Dedication

To General Jim Mattis and the Soldiers, Marines, Sailors, and Airmen who by their acuity, blood, sweat, and tears will protect this great Republic over the coming century.

PREFACE

IT IS PERHAPS UNUSUAL FOR AN AUTHOR TO SPELL OUT HOW HE OR she came to write a particular book, but in this case *America and the Future of War* has an interesting provenance. In the summer of 2015 I had attended a conference held by the Joint Staff on its preparatory work for issuing a new edition of an old document. Its title was to be and is *The Joint Operating Environment 2035*. The conference lasted four days and was an excruciating experience, at least for me. The master briefing came as close as I have ever seen the Joint Staff achieve its longed-for dream of an absolutely contentless briefing.

Having been one of the two authors of an earlier *Joint Operating Environment* (2008), which managed to annoy a number of foreign ambassadors—the Russian and Pakistani ambassadors in particular—and receive a complaint from a senior figure in the State Department that the document should have been classified because it disturbed foreign governments, I found the exercise appalling. There was nothing in it that gave the slightest hint of how subject to violent change the future will probably be. And it was clear that whatever criticisms and acid comments came from the floor, the Joint Staff intended to issue the document drawn from the briefing just as it was, based on assertions that its members were sure would offend no one.

There matters would have rested, and I would have returned to my home in Fairfax to work on the final edited pages and page proofs of the history of the Civil War that I had recently completed with my co-author Wayne Hsieh, as well as the model boats that have become a passion in my old age. Then fate intervened. Through my friend Frank Hoffman, I received an offer to write what is now titled *America and the Future of War* from Charles Smith, former ambassador and member of Paul Kennedy's grand strategy group at Yale. I would not say that I leaped at the opportunity, but I accepted largely because I believed that the product of the Joint Staff was going to be so abysmal and that at least the American military needed to face up to the challenges of the future.

The publication of *The Joint Operating Environment 2035* this summer (2016) has fully lived up to my expectations. In it, there is no serious analysis of major threats with the exception perhaps of technology; no discussion of the historical past; a complete disregard for potential "black swans"; and a general absence of any mention of the potential that a global economic collapse might have for the world's strategic stability and the capacity and willingness of the United States to support its defense establishment. It was, in every respect, a document of use only to insomniacs.

Thus, my decision to attempt to do what the Joint Staff was clearly unwilling or unable to do has led to this small book. It represents a contentious, argumentative view (mine alone) of the dark years that may well await the United States and its feckless leaders in the coming decades of the twenty-first century. It aims to outrage many and make most of the rest who bother to read it uncomfortable. They should be. As for me, if I have made more enemies, I remember fondly Machiavelli's comment: "More enemies, more honor!"

1

AN END TO WAR?

The hero becomes a thing dragged behind a chariot in the dust: . . . The bitterness of such a spectacle is offered us absolutely undiluted. No comforting fiction intervenes; no consoling prospect of immortality; and on the hero's head no washed-out halo of patriotism descends.

Simone Weil

You suppose that this war has been a criminal blunder and an exceptional horror; you imagine that before long reason will prevail, and all those inferior people who govern the world will be swept aside, and your own party will reform everything and remain always in office. You are mistaken. This war has given you your first glimpse of the ancient, fundamental, normal state of the world, your first taste of reality.

George Santayana

THIS SHORT STUDY EXAMINES WHAT HISTORY SUGGESTS ABOUT THE future possibilities of war as well as the place that thinking about conflict deserves in the articulation and course of American strategy in coming decades. As an historian, the author has no intention of providing predictions about the future; nor does he believe that social science trend analysis offers much that is useful in thinking about the future. The past does provide some glimmerings about what will be. But at best, history can only provide a guide to our interpreting of the unfolding of events and an intellectual framework for adapting to the uncomfortable shocks and traumas that the future will inevitably deliver to our doorstep, much of it in indigestible and unpalatable forms.

We might begin our examination with some thoughts about the potential for major conflicts to erupt over the course of coming decades. It has become popular in some areas of the social sciences to argue that the occurrence of war around the world has been in decline over the past half century and that that trend toward a more peaceful world will probably continue well into the future. Certainly the American academic landscape would suggest that those who populate its universities and colleges believe that to be the case. The number of institutions in the United States where a student can study military and diplomatic history, security studies, and even strategy seriously has declined almost to the point where one can count them on the fingers on two hands. At the same time the number of institutions hosting centers given to the study of conflict resolution has proliferated at a considerable rate.

One might have thought that the increasing violence throughout much of the Middle East, the onward march of Chinese claims on oceanic areas well beyond their shores, Russia's increasing resort to force in the Caucasus, the Ukraine, the Baltic states, not to mention Syria, among a host of other violent confrontations in other parts of the world might have given the intellectuals in America's academies pause. But in the gated communities of universities and colleges, where the real world is far from the minds and interests of those responsible for preparing new generations of Americans to deal with an unstable, uncertain, and fractious world, that is certainly not the case. Not surprisingly, the saying falsely attributed to Trotsky that "you may not be interested in war, but war is interested in you" remains far from their thoughts.

The purpose of this short study is to suggest that Mars, the God of War, is not yet dead and to examine the implications of that reality. It is, of course, dangerous for an historian to comment on the possible paths that the fates will unwind over coming decades. But history can and does suggest how to think about the future at least in preparing for its shocks. As the historian MacGregor Knox noted in the early 1990s:

> The owl of history is an evening bird. The past as a whole is unknowable; only at the end of the day do some of its outlines dimly emerge. The future cannot be known at all, and the past suggests that change is often radical and unforeseeable rather than incremental and predictable. Yet despite its many ambiguities, historical experience remains the only available guide both to the present and to the range of alternatives inherent in the future.[1]

Simply put, if you do not know where you have been (the past), then you do not know where you stand, and any road to the future will do. Thus, a perceptive understanding of the present based on historical knowledge is the first step to thinking about the future.

---

1. MacGregor Knox, "What History Can Tell Us about the 'New Strategic Environment,'" in Williamson Murray, ed., *Brassey's Mershon American Defense Annual, 1995–1996* (Washington, DC, 1996).

And of importance in understanding the past, even the recent past, is a considered and realistic understanding of the complex context within which historical events have occurred. In particular, as Knox underlines and this work will examine later, radical and unanticipated change is a major factor in the tangled course of human events. There is no indication such radical and unforeseen changes will not continue to confound those who believe that simple linear trends will determine man's fate in the coming decades.[2]

Those who have been prognosticating about the disappearance of war from the human condition have largely spent their time in rummaging through the past with little attention to the fact that trends are incapable of identifying the violent changes that so often wreck the comfortable illusion of progress. Nor are trends necessarily indicative of the context within which politics and strategic decision making take place. The most valuable lesson of a rich immersion in the past is that the only trend on which one might trust in thinking about the future is recognition of the infinite capacity of human action and reaction to trigger violent change. The most recent advocate of the "war is disappearing" theory is the Harvard psychologist Steven Pinker with his book, one that has gained considerable appeal.[3] In fact, what the good doctor has assembled is a collection of badly interpreted history, some discussion of literature that indicates that he was a recipient of what used to pass for an Ivy League education, and a discussion of irrelevant trends, because he lacks the historical

---

2. The most recent *Joint Operating Environment*, produced by the Joint Staff in the Pentagon, represents the worst kind of trend analysis. Its analysis is further muddied by bureaucratic prose that says little in the maximum number of words.

3. Steven Pinker, *The Better Angels of Our Nature: Why Violence Has Declined* (New York, 2011).

knowledge to understand the context within which those trends have taken place. As one critic has noted, he "seldom takes a long and careful look at the larger global and historical context in which decisions about war and peace are made. What we have instead is the rather nebulous and diffuse impact of changing sensibilities."[4]

Admittedly the period from 1945 to the present has displayed a distinct lack of a great power conflict on the battlefield. There was no World War III, although there were massive preparations for such a contingency. Nevertheless, the Cold War interlude reflected the context within which the struggle between the United States and its allies on one side and the Soviet Union and its allies on the other took place. The most obvious was the fact that the most costly war in human history in terms of casualties and destruction had just ended, a conflict which had seen somewhere in excess of 50 million human beings killed and every major city in Europe wrecked with the exception of Stockholm, Madrid, Geneva, Paris, and Prague. What kept the Cold War from then destroying what little remained of Western and North American civilization was the fact that Soviet and American leaders quite correctly concluded that they, too, would likely die should the contest turn hot with the planned use of nuclear weapons and that there would be precious little of their countries remaining in the aftermath of a nuclear holocaust.

Nevertheless, the absence of great power wars hardly suggested that peace had settled around the globe in the aftermath of the Second World War. Instead of a massive conflagration, innumerable smaller wars occurred to blot the landscapes of Asia and Africa. The

---

4. Quoted in Frank G. Hoffman and Ryan Neuhard, "No Wake for Ares," *Proceedings,* December 2015.

processes of decolonization provided a series of bitter wars: for the British, the Malayan and Kenyan insurgencies; for the French, war in Indochina, which the Americans followed a decade later in South Vietnam. The list continues on and on: the three wars between India and Pakistan; the Korean War; the Algerian revolution; the four Arab-Israeli wars; the collapse of the Congo into interminable conflict after the withdrawal of the Belgians; and even the short, bitter war between Britain and Argentina over the Falklands. The collapse of the Portuguese Empire in the early 1970s resulted in the nasty civil wars in Angola and Mozambique, in which Soviet and American proxies delightedly participated. None of these vicious conflicts were on the level of the great world wars, but they certainly underlined that peace was hardly at hand, even with the restraining hands on nuclear triggers, at least in those areas where the great powers believed their most important interests were in play.

The miracle of the peaceful Soviet collapse then supposedly resulted in what some pundits termed America's unipolar moment. Accompanying that decade's intellectual themes was Francis Fukuyama's *The End of History and the Last Man*, a more sophisticated work than its title suggested, but one that reflected the American belief that history was irrelevant. Given the fact of America's overwhelming military preponderance in the post–Cold War period, one that Saddam Hussein was kind enough to test with his invasion of Kuwait, there were few, except for Arab religious fanatics, who were willing to test the reality of overwhelming American power. But where the Americans were unwilling to involve themselves, such as in the Balkans, Somalia, and Rwanda, ancient hatreds reappeared with murderous results. What now appears to be occurring, at least in terms of President Obama's strategic policies, is that America's preponderance of military power and its willingness to use that power are beginning to unravel, a situation which some with little, or no, understanding of the role of the American military in maintaining stability or peace will undoubtedly find attractive.

THOUGHTS ON THE ARRIVAL OF PEACE IN THE PAST

Ironically, given their disinterest in any deep study in history, contemporary commentators are not alone in mistaking the temporary absence of conflict as heralding the arrival of a new age where wars are fewer. Over the past centuries, numerous politicians and pundits have proclaimed that the incidents of human conflict were on the decline, arguments that echo today's pronouncements. In 1792, a decade after the conclusion of peace between Britain and France, the great British statesman, William Pitt the Younger, declaimed in the House of Commons: "unquestionably there never was a time in the history of this country when, from the situation in Europe, we might more reasonably expect fifteen years of peace, than we may at the present moment."[5] He could not have been more wrong about the future.

Within a matter of months Britain and the other major European powers had declared war on Revolutionary France and embarked on a series of wars against the French and their allies that would last for almost a quarter century. As Carl von Clausewitz noted, the

---

5. Quoted in Colin Gray, *Another Bloody Century, Future Warfare* (London, 2005).

next 23 years of warfare resulted in revolutionary changes and conflict. The cause was the fact that

> [i]n 1793 a force appeared and beggared all imagination. Suddenly war again became the business of the people—a people of thirty millions, all of whom considered themselves citizens. . . . The people became a participant in war; instead of governments and armies as heretofore, the full weight of the nation was thrown into the balance. The resources and efforts now available for use surpassed all conventional limits; nothing now impeded the vigor with which war could be waged, and consequently the opponents of France faced the utmost peril.[6]

Why did Pitt get it so wrong? There are two possible explanations: The first is that, while nearly one-third of the previous years in the eighteenth century had involved wars between the major European governments, those conflicts, as Clausewitz suggests, had remained limited to cabinet wars. The forces involved had been relatively small, while the combatants had never really aimed at the complete overthrow of their opponents. The second factor was that France, Britain's great continental enemy during the previous century, appeared to be in a state of collapse with the king's authority in dispute and the nation's military forces dissolving as the other European powers watched. The explosion that followed after 1789, which was as unexpected to contemporary observers as was the collapse of the Soviet Union in 1989, quite literally blew up the map

---

6. Carl von Clausewitz, *On War*, translated and edited by Michael Howard and Peter Paret (Princeton, NJ, 1976), p. 593.

of Europe for the next quarter of a century. As Pitt commented after Napoleon's crushing defeat of Allied forces at the Battle of Austerlitz in 1805, "[r]oll up that map; it will not be needed these ten years."

In 1815, a Europe, exhausted by the French Revolutionary and Napoleonic Wars, entered one of the most surprising periods in its history: a near century of peace. There were, of course, relatively minor squabbles: the Crimean War, the Danish War of 1864, the Austro-Prussian War of 1866, and the Franco-Prussian War of 1870–1871.[7] Only the last conflict threatened to get out of hand as both the Prusso-Germans and the French unleashed the fervor of nationalism in service of their war efforts. But the disastrous defeats Napoleon III's imperial army had suffered in the conflict's first month prevented the French from putting together effective military forces. More than forty years of peace then followed the Franco-Prussian War, as the Europeans created the first great period of globalization, a period that incorporated much of the world into an economic interdependence and that provided an economic expansion never before seen in history. Admittedly, if there were some gross inequalities, the trickle-down impact of capitalistic economics provided for the working class in a fashion never before seen.

---

7. There was, of course, the American Civil War, but that occurred far from Europe's shores, while the appearance of its armies, which possessed none of the spit and polish of European armies, misled most Europeans as to its warning. As the chief of Prussia's Great General Staff commented, there was nothing to be learned from a war waged by militias. See chapter of this study for an examination of the American Civil War's importance for understanding the course of Western war.

Nevertheless, the sustained period of relative peace was not the result of stability underlying the relations among the powers. Rather, from the "war in sight" crisis of 1875, Otto von Bismarck, the chancellor of the new German Empire, recognized how dangerously exposed his creation, the unified German state, was in the center of Europe. For the next fifteen years the iron chancellor managed the instability of the complex interrelations of Europe's great power politics with enormous skill. Confronted with the considerable hostility of the Austro-Hungarian and Russian empires as well as the dangerously unstable political situation in the Balkans, the German chancellor kept diplomatic and political differences from spilling over into a disastrous conflict. However, his removal by the new kaiser, Wilhelm II, led to the slow but sure destruction of the Bismarckian system as well as the appearance of a far more aggressive foreign policy by his successors. But for two more decades Europe remained at peace; and the period before the disastrous outbreak of war in 1914 saw unprecedented economic progress that expanded far beyond Europe's frontiers. Nevertheless, in the largest sense one might note that statesmen, governments, and even historians mistake peace for stability; and the period after 1871 was a period in which instability churned underneath the appearance of a peaceful Europe.

In 1909 an English journalist, Norman Angell, published a pamphlet titled "Europe's Optical Illusion," which the following year he expanded into a book, *The Grand Illusion*. Angell's arguments made a great deal of sense, at least if mankind consisted entirely of rational actors. Quite simply, he argued that the economies and finances of the European powers, and much of the rest of the globe, had become so intertwined that a major war would cause a catastrophic economic collapse. And certainly the economic benefits of that interdependence had had a favorable impact on Europe's population as well as on those global extensions of Europe such as the United States, Canada, Australia, and Argentina, among others. The synopsis of the 1913 edition of Angell's book suggested: "For a modern nation to add to its territory no more adds to the wealth of the people of such nation than it would add to the wealth of Londoners if the City of London were to annex the county of Hertford."[8] Thus, war and military power made no sense in the modern globalized world, at least to those who thought in a similar fashion.

In retrospect, Angell's argument was right. The problem was that it ignored the nature of Germany's leadership and the place of the Reich's military in German society. German leaders in the first years of the twentieth century and a considerable portion of their population were rational actors within an entirely different *Weltanschauung*, a German worldview that posited war as a fundamental necessity to protect the Reich's position in the center of Europe. In the 1960s, the German historian Fritz Fischer argued that Germany's leaders had unleashed the First World War deliberately. After historians had spent reams of paper and ink on Fischer's thesis, the general view has emerged that while the Germans may not have deliberately set out to cause a great world war, they certainly were the major instigators. The suggestion that several recent historians have made that the war largely resulted from miscalculations rather than deliberate actions, particularly of the Germans, simply does not hold water.

---

8. Norman Angell, *The Great Illusion* (New York, 1913), pp. xxi.

It was not just that there were considerable mass demonstrations—minimized by several recent historians—but the great majority of Germany's intellectual elite welcomed the outbreak of war. As Mac-Gregor Knox has pointed out:

> Max Weber, with fewer illusions than most about Germany's prospects, nevertheless wrote to a friend that "*however* it turns out, *this war is great and wonderful*." Thomas Mann, the archetypal literary *Bildungsbürger*, wrote that the poets knew it: war meant "purification, liberation, and immense hope. What inspired them was not the hope of victory 'but the war itself, as divine visitation, as moral necessity.'" The [German] poets indeed worked overtime; by one perhaps extreme contemporary estimate the German people produced 1.5 million war poems in August 1914, an average of 50,000 a day. . . . In the tradition of Marx and Engels the SPD [the socialist party] took up with enthusiasm the struggle against the "Cossack bestialities" and "collapse, annihilation, and nameless misery" that threatened from the Muscovite despotism to Germany's east.[9]

There was, of course, an element of miscalculation, as there always is in international affairs. Not only do statesmen often misestimate the nature of the other, but because of differences in language, culture, background, and education, they inevitably find it difficult to understand how their opponents will act. Moreover, unlike historians who have decades and centuries to argue about

---

9. MacGregor Knox, *To the Threshold of Power, 1922/23, Origins and Dynamics of the Fascist and National Socialist Dictatorships*, vol. 1 (Cambridge, 2007), pp. 170–171.

what should have been done, political and military leaders are under the enormous pressure of events so fast-moving that they have almost no time for reflection or calculation. None of this makes war any less likely. In his memoirs about the First World War, Winston Churchill put the immediate events that resulted in the war in the following terms:

> One arises from the study of the causes of the Great War with a prevailing sense of the defective control of individuals upon world fortunes. It has been well said that "There is always more error than design in human affairs." The limited minds of the ablest men, their disputed authority, the climate of opinion in which they dwell, their transient and partial contributions to the mighty problem, that problem itself so far beyond their compass, so vast in scale and detail, so changing in its aspects—all this must surely be considered. . . . Events . . . got onto certain lines and no one could get them off again.[10]

Nevertheless, as Churchill then notes, "Germany clanked obstinately, recklessly, awkwardly towards the crater and dragged us all in with her."[11] Ironically, the hard lessons of the First World War seem to have never caught the attention of most of those who made strategic policy in the interwar period.

In spite of the clear warning as to Germany's vulnerable position, Adolf Hitler and the German leadership embarked on the invasion of Poland on September 1, 1939, with some trepidation, but fully

---

10. Winston S. Churchill, *The World Crisis* (London, 1931), p. 6.
11. Ibid., p. 6.

aware of the risks they were taking. In a rational world, in which one calculated one's experiences with some care, the Second World War should never have occurred. Certainly the catastrophic human and economic losses of the last war should have provided more than sufficient evidence that even the victors had won little of real value. That was the conclusion that many in Britain and France, particularly among the elites, drew from the catastrophic war that had bled their nations white. They now fervently believed that strategic issues and historical precedents were no longer relevant in this new world where statesmen no longer thought in terms of war.

Such attitudes were, of course, the major intellectual drivers that underpinned the British policy of appeasement toward Nazi Germany. Reinforced by a wave of some of the greatest literature on war ever written, all of it understandably deeply hostile to the war, British leaders could simply not believe that Hitler, a combat veteran, much less the German people, would voluntarily initiate another great war.[12] The result was muddled thinking to an extraordinary extent. A "critic" noted in the *New Statesman* in 1936 in the early days of the struggle against Franco and his Spanish Fascists: "I see no intellectual difficulty in at once working for the victory of the Spanish people and in being glad of the growing pacifist movement in England."[13] From our perspective, it is indeed surprising that a publisher would reissue Norman Angell's *The Great Illusion* to considerable enthusiasm in Britain and the United States in 1937. Yet,

---

12. The greatest of these memoirs of the war and the least wrapped up in political bitterness is Frederic Manning's *The Middle Parts of Fortune* (London, 1929).

13. *New Statesman,* 22 August 1936.

from the perspective of the time it seemed simply inconceivable that any modern power, particularly one like Germany that was so vulnerable in economic terms, would be willing to embark on a major war.[14]

In the end Prime Minister Neville Chamberlain's strategic policy rested on a best-case analysis of Hitler's intentions with the disastrous result of pandering to German bad behavior, while at the same time minimizing Britain's rearmament. Chamberlain and his fellow politicians lacked any understanding of the culture, context, and aspirations of their immediate neighbor across the North Sea. In the midst of the 1938 crisis over Czechoslovakia, a crisis entirely instigated by the Germans, the British ambassador in Berlin, Sir Nevile Henderson, wrote to Chamberlain's foreign secretary, Lord Halifax, concerning the mediator, Lord Runciman, whom the government had sent to Central Europe to defuse the growing crisis between Germany and Czechoslovakia:

> Personally I just sit and pray for one thing, namely that Lord Runciman will live up to the role of [an] impartial British statesman. I cannot believe that he will allow himself to be influenced by ancient history or even arguments about strategic frontiers and economics in preference to high moral principles. The great and courageous game which you and the Prime Minister are playing [namely to surrender Czechoslovakia to the tender mercies of Nazi Germany] will be lost in my humble opinion if

---

14. For the Third Reich's economic and strategic vulnerabilities, see particularly Williamson Murray, *The Change in the European Balance of Power, 1938–1939; The Path to Ruin* (Princeton, NJ, 1984), ch. 1.

[Runciman] does not come out on this side of the higher moral principles for which in fact the British Empire really stands.[15]

In fact, the First World War had certainly not persuaded the German elite, as well as the Nazis, of the notion that war was necessarily a bad thing. The greatest German literary figure of the First World War, Ernst Jünger, was anything but a pacifist. A veteran of nearly four years on the Western Front, storm troop officer, wounded a number of times, and winner of the *pour le mérite* (the highest combat decoration in the German Army), Jünger believed the war had been an ennobling experience, one that every generation should experience. The contrast between German literature and British literature could have been more graphic. But the larger problem lay deeper than simply a literary difference in the interpretations of the war. Although none of the other major German war memoirs came close to the quality of Jünger's writings, they shared with him a bloody-minded enthusiasm for the war. In every respect Erich Maria Remarque's *All Quiet on the Western Front* was an anomaly, far more popular in Britain and the United States than Germany.

The German explanation for their military defeat in fall 1918 was not that they had taken on the whole world and lost, which was the sensible explanation in strategic terms. Instead, almost immediately after the Germans had signed the armistice ending the war, the national narrative became that the home front had stabbed the German Army, unbroken and unbeaten on the Western Front, in the back. It did not take long for those on the right to identify those

---

15. *Documents on British Foreign Policy*, 3rd. Ser., vol. 2, Doc 390, 6.8.38, letter from Sir Nevile Henderson to Lord Halifax.

responsible as the Jews and the communists. Ironically, in terms of who would dominate the narrative, Friedrich Ebert, leader of the Social Democratic Party (SPD) and soon to be the new president of Germany's defeated Reich, proclaimed to the returning Guards Division in Berlin in December 1918 that "No enemy has subdued you."[16] Thus, the stab-in-the-back legend was not simply the result of the efforts of Erich Ludenorff and the right-wing demagogues who sprouted in the Weimar Republic to ignore the fact that the German Army was confronting a disastrous military collapse and defeat by October 1918, but a national consensus that the army had supposedly not been defeated as well.

The result was also a narrative that believed Germany was not the major driver of the outbreak of war in 1914, that her military had participated in few if any atrocities, and that the Reich had won the war only to be robbed of the fruits of victory by the November criminals (as Hitler characterized those who had signed the armistice in 1918).[17] If the French, British, and American polities believed that civilized states no longer considered the employment of military force, that was certainly not how most Germans viewed international relations. Hitler's assumption of power in Germany in January 1933 served only to exacerbate national tendencies. Even before he had come to power, Hitler had made clear his intentions.[18] The title of his victory speech in September 1930 after the Nazi Party

---

16. Knox, *To the Threshold of Power,* vol. 1, p. 198.

17. In the period between early August and September 1914, the German Army shot 6,000 civilians supposedly in response for attacks carried out by *franc-tireurs*. For German atrocities during this period, see particularly John Horne and Alan Kramer, *German Atrocities, 1914: A History of Denial* (New Haven, CT, 2001).

18. There was, of course, *Mein Kampf*, but few took it seriously as a statement of Hitler's future aims once he had achieved power.

had achieved its astonishing rise in the parliamentary elections for the *Reichstag* was, "after victory, tighten your chin strap." He was even more explicit in his speech: "When today so many preach that we are entering an age of peace, I can only say: my dear fellows, *you have badly misinterpreted the horoscope of the age, for it points not to peace, but to war as never before.*"[19] Almost inevitably because they were incapable of understanding the German response to defeat, the leaders and population of the democracies refused to recognize the harsh realities of a Nazi regime bent on destroying the international order.

That refusal by the democracies resulted from their preconceptions as well as their inability to recognize that their own definitions of cause and effect and rationality were culturally determined and not universal. Their deep-seated belief that war was inconceivable in the modern world led directly to the surrender of Czechoslovakia to the tender mercies of Hitler's monstrous regime at Munich. Churchill, not surprisingly, caught the full strategic and moral consequences of that triumph of appeasement in his early October 1938 speech before the House of Commons. The British people "should know," Churchill warned,

> that we have sustained a defeat without a war, the consequences of which will travel far with us along our road; they should know that we have passed an awful milestone in our history, when the whole equilibrium of Europe has been deranged, and that the terrible words have for the time being been pronounced against

---

19. Ibid., vol. 1, pp. 360–61.

the Western Democracies: "Thou art weighed in the balance and
found wanting. And do not suppose that this is the end. This is
only the beginning of the reckoning. This is only the first sip, the
first foretaste of a bitter cup."[20]

Churchill's speech received deep disapproval from those members
present.

THE DARK WARNINGS OF THE PAST

Two years after the Munich crisis and immediately after the catastrophic fall of France in May 1940, the French philosopher and
activist Simone Weil wrote a dark and prophetic essay on Homer's
Iliad, that ancient Greek epic poem on the war between the Greek
warrior tribes and the Trojans. Her essay was a bleak description of
what had just happened and what was soon to come. In her essay she
noted that

The true hero, the true subject, the center of the *Iliad* is force.
Force employed by man, force that enslaves man, force before
which man's flesh shrinks away. . . . For those who considered
that force, thanks to progress, would soon be a thing of the past,
the *Iliad* could appear as a historical document; for others, whose
powers of recognition are more acute and who perceive force,

---

20. Quoted in Winston S. Churchill, *The Second World War*, vol. 1, *The Gather-
ing Storm* (Boston, 1948), pp. 327–28.

today as yesterday, at the very center of human history, the *Iliad* is the purest and the loveliest of mirrors.[21]

Weil's essay underlined the fatal consequences that had attended those who had so casually dismissed the threat that German military force had represented as it grew year by year after Hitler had arrived in power. That misjudgment lay in an incapacity and an unwillingness to recognize how far removed their understanding of the world was from that of the leaders of Nazi Germany, or for that matter much of the German population. From their point of view, Hitler had to be a reasonable politician, although perhaps somewhat bombastic. After all, was not he a veteran of the terrible slaughter of the Western Front and would not he have drawn similar conceptions as they did? For them the *Iliad* represented only literature, echoing a long-lost civilization. For the Nazis, however, as Weil so intuitively understood, the *Iliad*'s understanding of force and violence was part and parcel of their worldview without any sense of Homer's dark portrayal of the dismal psychological consequences of war's impact on the human psyche.

For all of the attempts of the Western world to tie its civilization to that of the Greeks—at least until the politically correct academics began their assault on the literary heritage of dead white males—there has always been a fundamental disconnect between how the ancients regarded the future and the past, and how the moderns considered the relationship between the two. The great classicist Bernard Knox once noted that "the early Greek imagina-

---

21. Simone Weil, "The Iliad, or the Poem of Force," *Chicago Review*, 18:2 (1965), p. 5.

tion envisaged the past and the present as in front of us—we can see them. The future invisible is behind us. . . . Paradoxical though it may sound to the modern ear, this image of our journey through time may be truer to reality than the medieval and modern feeling that we face the future as we make our way forward into it."[22] That, of course, suggests why the moderns have made such herculean efforts in the social sciences in the hopeless task of trying to bring clarity to thinking about the future, an effort that is inherently unpredictable.

That fundamental difference underlines the vast gulf between the great Greek historian Thucydides and his view of the world and that of modern social scientists and too many historians. In his opening paragraphs he made clear that "it will be enough for me . . . if these words of mine are judged useful by those who want to understand clearly the events which happened in the past and which (human nature being what it is) will at some time or other and in much the same ways, be repeated in the future."[23] But there is nothing predictive about Thucydides's account of the terrible events that transpired in the three-decade-long Peloponnesian War. He fully lays out only the nature of human behavior in the interplay of events that provide his future readers some sense of how human beings will act under similar circumstances.

At the heart of all human political actions, according to Thucydides, lies his famous triptych: "security, honor, and self-interest."[24] In

---

22. Bernard Knox, *Backing into the Future: The Classical Tradition and Its Renewal* (New York, 1994), pp. 11–12.

23. Thucydides, *History of the Peloponnesian War,* translated by Rex Warner (London, 1954), p. 48.

24. Ibid., p. 80.

explaining their position to the Spartan assembly in the run-up to war, Thucydides records that the Athenian diplomats defended their control over their maritime empire in the Aegean:

> We have done nothing extraordinary, nothing contrary to human nature in accepting an empire when it was offered to us and then in refusing to give it up. . . . And we were not the first to act in this way. Far from it. It has always been a rule that the weak should be subject to the strong; and besides, we consider that we are worthy of our power. . . . Those who really deserve praise are the people who, while human enough to enjoy power, nevertheless pay more attention to justice than they are compelled to do by their situation.[25]

Thus, like Weil, Thucydides believed that force, in one form or another, underlies the action of all states. Great powers may pay attention to issues such as justice and humane behavior in their interactions with the world, but that is only because they choose to do so, and because such behavior does not threaten or undermine their position or fundamental interests.

It is the last sentence of the above quotation that is particularly applicable to how Americans need think about the future of the United States. In its use of its power and particularly its military power, its leaders must pay some attention to the issues of justice as well as its self-interest. To do that represents an exceedingly difficult task. But not to recognize that force *must* form an integral and crucial part of the pursuit of some order is to ignore history—

---

25. Ibid., p. 80.

our own as well as that of others. It is to place our trust in the hope that other nations and entities will act in what Americans view as a reasonable fashion, a belief and assumption that too many have placed their hopes in with disastrous results for themselves and their allies.

In even blunter fashion than in their discussion with the Spartans, the Athenians replied to the Melian negotiators who attempted to deflect the former's demand that they join the Athenian empire with reference to justice and the Gods:

> So far as the favor of the Gods is concerned, we think that we have as much right to that as you have. Our aims and our actions are perfectly consistent with the beliefs men hold about the Gods and with the principles which govern their own conduct. Our opinion of the Gods and our knowledge of men leads us to conclude that it is a general and necessary law of nature to rule whatever one can. This is not a law that we have made ourselves, nor were we the first to act upon it when it was made. We found it already in existence, and we shall leave it to exist forever among those who come after us.[26]

For those then who look at the past with dispassion, there is nothing in the history of the past 2,400 years, since Thucydides wrote his history, to suggest that this dark and pessimistic view of man's fate did not represent an accurate prediction of what was to come. The basic problem is that, as Michael Howard has suggested, war has been a constant companion of mankind's course, while to

---

26. Ibid., p. 404.

all intents and purposes peace is a modern invention. "Archeological, anthropological, as well as all surviving documentary evidence indicates that war, armed conflict between organized political groups, has been the universal norm in human history."[27] The problem then is set for America's strategic future. Its stark choice is that on one hand most American leaders hope that human nature has radically changed, as professor Pinker believes, and thus believe the nation can diminish both its military power as well as its willingness to use that power. On the other hand, there are those who believe that its responsibility as a great power demands that it recognize the nature of the world in which we live—a world where force, power, and even war remain driving factors in the fabric of international relations.

---

27. Michael Howard, *The Invention of Peace & the Reinvention of War* (London, 2002), p. 1.

2

THE NATURE AND
CHARACTER OF WAR

1. *War is an art, a free and creative activity founded on scientific principles.*
   It makes the very highest demands on the human personality.
2. *The conduct of war is subject to continual development. New weapons*
   dictate ever-changing forms. Their appearance must be anticipated and
   their influence evaluated . . .
3. *Combat situations are of an unlimited variety. They change frequently*
   and suddenly and seldom can be assessed in advance. Incalculable
   elements often have a decisive influence. One's own will is pitted
   against the independent will of the enemy. Friction and error are daily
   occurrences.

Truppenführung

IN 1990 THE UNITED STATES CONFRONTED THE REALITY THAT IT might be necessary to employ its military forces to eject an Iraqi Army, supposedly battle-hardened by an eight-year war with the

Iranians, from Kuwait.[1] In the Congress, the media, and even portions of the military, lurid tales circulated about the tens of thousands of casualties US forces would suffer, if it were to come to a military confrontation. Commentators, who should have known better, referred again and again to the Vietnam War, as if US forces were going to repeat that dismal experience against Saddam Hussein's forces. Considering what actually was to happen, it is difficult to remember how pervasive such views were.

And then came the war. The air campaign began on the night of January 15, 1991, with the loss of a single aircraft, whereas the prewar prediction was that the US-led coalition would lose 35 aircraft. In that operation, coalition air power destroyed Iraq's air defense system, equipped with the most modern French and Soviet equipment. A month of steady pounding followed against targets in Iraq and the Kuwaiti theater of operations. Aircraft losses were minimal, while the few precision weapons the Americans possessed inflicted terrible damage on Iraq's military and its infrastructure. Slightly over a month later, on February 24, the ground campaign began in spite of dire warnings about the losses coalition ground forces, particularly those of the United States, would suffer. Again, events proved the so-called experts wrong. At location 73 Easting in southern Iraq, a squadron of Abrams M1A1 tanks and Bradley armored personnel carriers destroyed an entire Iraqi armored battalion without the loss of a single vehicle or soldier. As the remainder of the 2nd Armored Cavalry Regiment came online, the destruction

---

1. Portions of this chapter have been adapted from a chapter titled "Thinking about Revolutions in Warfare" that the author and MacGregor Knox wrote in a book we edited: *The Dynamics of Military Revolution, 1300–2050* (Cambridge, 2000).

of the remainder of Saddam's elite Tawakana Republican Guards Division followed in short order. The ground campaign was over in 100 hours, and only the mishandling of the immediate postwar period by American political and military leaders prevented the fall of Saddam's murderous regime.

The months that followed the war were euphoric for America's political and military leaders. With the collapse of the Soviet Union occurring almost concurrently, some pundits and academics announced the arrival of the unipolar moment.[2] For the American military, there appeared no serious challenger on the horizon. In the midst of the enthusiasm, the Office of Net Assessment, led by the redoubtable Andrew Marshall, who had been in that office since 1972 and who would not retire until January 2015, suggested that a major revolution in military affairs had occurred over the past several decades in technological and conceptual developments.[3] Marshall, as always, was careful with his prognostication; he suggested that events in the Gulf War represented only the first stage of what he initially called a military technological revolution. And he added that the American military were only as far in developing their revolution as the British had been with their use of tanks in the Battle of Cambrai in November 1917, which represented a signal victory over the German Army as well as the arrival of armored fighting vehicles as significant weapons of war.

---

2. Charles Krauthammer, "The Unipolar Moment," *Foreign Affairs,* vol. 70, 1990–1991, pp. 23–33.

3. For an examination of Marshall's career, see Andrew F. Krepinevich and Barry D. Watts, *The Last Warrior: Andrew Marshall and the Shaping of Modern American Defense Strategy* (New York, 2015).

To a considerable extent, Marshall was drawing on Soviet observations over the past several decades on developments in the United States with leading-edge technologies such as stealth and precision. The Soviets' first inkling of the increasing sophistication of the American military had come with "Linebackers I and II," the air campaigns against the North Vietnamese in 1972. During those air campaigns the US Air Force dropped in excess of 27,000 laser-guided munitions (LGBs). The attacks wrecked targets such as the Paul Doumer and Thanh Hóa bridges near Hanoi in a matter of a few raids, whereas three years of raids during "Rolling Thunder" (1965–1968) had failed to drop either span at a heavy cost in US aircraft lost.

But it is probable that the Soviets were even more worried about the fact that American LGBs had devastated the North Vietnamese armies attacking South Vietnam, particularly the logistical lines supporting the conventional ground operations they were conducting against the South Vietnamese as well as their command and control centers. Throughout the 1970s, the American military worked on the development of stealth and further refined precision-guided munitions. In 1982, during the invasion of Lebanon, the Soviets watched as the Israelis, equipped largely with American weapons, destroyed the Syrian air defense systems in the Bekaa Valley, a defensive array equipped with the most up-to-date of their systems. At the same time the Israel Defense Forces shot down 80 Syrian aircraft without the loss of a single aircraft. The depressing results led Marshal Nikolai Ogarkov, chief of the Soviet general staff, to comment to a Soviet newspaper reporter in 1984 that the technological advances within the US military "make possible to sharply increase (by at least an order of magnitude) the destructive potential of conventional weapons, bringing them closer, so to speak, to weapons of mass destruction [nuclear] in terms of [their] effectiveness."[4]

Ironically, the Americans had spent relatively little time in the 1970s and 1980s in assessing the operational implications of their technological developments. In fact, they had placed so little emphasis on the increasing sophistication of their precision weapons that only the F-111Es and F-117s of the vast numbers of tactical aircraft in the US inventory had fully trained crews capable of utilizing precision-guided weapons at the start of the conflict. Not surprisingly, that state of affairs changed in the aftermath of the success of American military forces against Saddam's overmatched army and air forces in 1991. In fact, technology became the mantra of the scaled-down, but still enormously capable, American military forces in the period after the Gulf War.

A number of pundits and senior officers seized on the initial term that Marshall's Office of Net Assessment had utilized: that the United States was in the midst of a "military-technical revolution," which is how the Soviets had characterized US military developments. Too sophisticated to succumb to the belief that only technology was driving what was occurring, Marshall shifted the terminology of his office to "revolution in military affairs," a definition broader in scope. The Office of Net Assessment then turned to a number of historians to examine past periods in history where major changes in military affairs had occurred. All of those studies underlined that

4. Interview with Marshal of the Soviet Union Nikolai V. Orgarkov, "The Defense of Socialism: Experience of History and the Present Day," *Krasnnaya zvezda*, 1st edition, 9 May 1984.

while technology usually played a role in such periods of change, other factors, such as new doctrine and improved concepts, more often than not, were the critical factors in striking improvement in military capabilities.

However, Marshall's nuanced approach had little impact on the host of true believers that now sprang up throughout the department of defense. They accepted the new terminology, but the "revolution in military affairs" to them was simply a matter of technological change, and the more rapid the better. History, of course, had no role in their conceptions, because they argued that the "revolution in military affairs" had made the past irrelevant to those marching forward into a bright, modern future. The claims of what was possible were indeed extraordinary. Leading general and flag officers, especially in the air force and navy, emphasized that the technological changes cascading into America's military forces made the evidence of the past and warnings of theorists like Clausewitz about the general prevalence of friction irrelevant for understanding future military developments.

Foremost among these exponents of the technological future was Admiral Bill Owens, vice-chairman of the joint chiefs of staff in the mid-1990s. Among the many claims that Owens made during this period were the following:

> Technology could enable US military forces in the future to lift the "fog of war . . ." Battlefield dominant awareness—the ability to see and understand everything on the battlefield—might be possible.
>
> When you look at areas such as information warfare, intelligence, surveillance, reconnaissance, and command and control,

you see a system of systems coming together that will allow us to dominate battlefield awareness for years to come. . . . And while some people say there will always be a "fog of war," I know quite a lot about these programs.

The emerging system of systems promises the capacity to use military force without the same risks as before. It suggests we will dissipate the "fog of war."[5]

But Owens was hardly the only senior officer treading down the path of technological monism. Not surprisingly, the air force, always an enthusiastic supporter of new technologies and eager to escape from the gloomy lessons of the past, enthusiastically supported the idea of a "military-technical revolution." Its *New World Vistas,* sponsored by the air force's chief of staff, suggested in the mid-1990s that "[t]he power of new information systems will lie in their ability to correlate data automatically and rapidly from many sources to form a complete picture of the operational area, whether it will be of the battlefield or the site of a mobility operation."[6] In 1995, a senior army general even announced to a group of marine officers that "the digitation of the battlefield spelled the end of Clausewitz's relevance to the understanding of war."[7]

------

5. William Owens quoted in respectively: Thomas Duffy, "Breakthrough Could Give Forces Total Command of Future Battlefield," *Inside the Navy,* 23 January 1995; Peter Grier, "Preparing for 21st Century Information War," *Government Executive* (August 1995); and his own, "System of Systems," *Joint Forces Quarterly* (January 1996).

6. US Air Force, *New World Vistas: Air and Space Power in the 21st Century* (Washington, DC, 1995).

7. The author was present when a senior army general made the statement in the mid-1990s.

Simply put, the new *Weltanschauung* represented in its essence a belief that American technological superiority would allow US military forces to achieve quick, easy victories over any opponent with relatively few casualties. In particular, such beliefs posited that ground forces, which invariably in war suffer the heaviest casualties, would have to play only a minimal role. In his 2002 downsizing of US forces scheduled for the impending invasion of Iraq, Donald Rumsfeld, the new secretary of defense in 2001, aimed at achieving that goal. He firmly believed that technologically superior US forces could achieve a swift decisive victory, which would allow the United States to withdraw almost as quickly as it had defeated the Iraqis. Thus, his willingness to cut substantial forces from deployment plans for the 2003 offensive against Iraq. His decision to cut off the flow of reinforcements after Saddam's regime collapsed represented his estimate of a new American way of war. Ironically, in spite of the political distance between Rumsfeld and the current president, Barack Obama, the latter's massive use of drones, precision air-strikes, and special operations forces raids represents a similar reliance on technology in order to avoid the political and financial costs involved in the use of ground forces.[8]

Luckily for the initial conventional invasion of 2003, Saddam played into US hands by attempting to meet American forces out in the open. A few of the dictator's advisers had warned Saddam that such an approach would result in a rapid and complete defeat for the Iraqi Army; instead, they urged him to concentrate his forces defensively in the cities and force the Americans to dig the Iraqis out in

---

8. For a critique of President Obama's strategy, see Colin Dueck, *The Obama Doctrine: American Grand Strategy Today* (Oxford, 2015).

the complexities of their urban terrain. Saddam refused to listen, and the conventional invasion succeeded within slightly more than a month. The Americans appeared to have gained a swift, decisive victory. They certainly dominated the battle space, but the so-called advantages of "information dominance" proved somewhat dubious. In fact the advocates of a supposed "information revolution" soon discovered that rather than bringing a radical military and controllable result, the supposed revolution had consequences and implications that were largely unpredictable. Even in the period of American success, as US forces wrecked Saddam's ill-trained forces, the head of intelligence for coalition forces moaned that "he was drowning in information." The subtext, of course, was that neither he nor his staff were capable of dealing with the masses of intelligence flowing into his headquarters from his sensors.

In conventional terms, the success of US arms was impressive, but events soon proved that Rumsfeld's approach meant that the coalition had too few troops on the ground to handle the insurgency that soon spiraled out of control. Nor did all of the technological sophistication of the new model American military prove capable of handling many of the political and tactical problems raised by Iraqi insurgents who hid among a population, the culture and language of which the Americans had little preparation to handle. So ill-prepared did some of the US ground forces and their commanders prove in handling the insurgents over the next three years that one could conclude only that the American military had forgotten the lessons of the Vietnam War, if they had ever bothered to learn them.

What had gone wrong, then, with the claims that Admiral Owens and others had made in the debacle that followed the 2003 invasion?

In simple terms, ignorant of history or for that matter of military theory, they had missed the fact that there were two inseparable sides of the Janus-like face of war. As the marine corps' basic doctrinal manual, *Warfighting* (one of the few doctrinal statements by the US military worth reading) suggests, "[w]ar is both timeless and ever changing."[9] The fundamental nature of war itself has remained constant throughout history. Friction and the fog of war represent constants because nonlinear factors drive the universe in which we live. The great British historian Sir Michael Howard noted in a more sophisticated fashion that "[a]fter all historical allowances have been made for historical differences, wars still resemble each other than they resemble any other human activity. All are fought, as Clausewitz insisted, in a special element of danger and fear and confusion. In all large bodies of men are trying to impose their will on one another by violence, and in all events occur which are inconceivable in any other field of experience."[10]

Thus, one cannot boil complex human interactions that occur in war and that involve innumerable events and decisions, involving the deaths of huge numbers of human beings, which in its simplest terms is what war is, down to simple equations. The enemy always gets a vote; moreover, he will more often than not adapt in ways that are unexpected and confounding to our assumptions. Thus, there are aspects of human conflict that will not change no matter what advances in technology or computing power may occur. Nor are technological advances and computing power necessarily able to

---

9. US Marine Corps, *Warfighting* (Washington, DC, 1997), p. 17.

10. Michael Howard, *The Causes of War and Other Essays* (London, 1984), p. 214.

handle the manifold implications of an enemy's capacity to adapt in unexpected ways.

On the other hand, the *character* of war, particularly as it has come to be shaped by the technological and social changes that have molded the Western world since the sixteenth century, has changed over the centuries. And over the past two centuries, it appears to be changing at an increasingly rapid pace with technology and scientific advances providing new and more complex weapons, means of production, communications, and sensors, and myriad other inventions, all capable of altering the character of the battle space in unexpected fashions. We will now turn to these two aspects of war, aspects that are essential to an understanding of war in the twenty-first century.

THE FUNDAMENTAL NATURE OF WAR

We might begin our discussion on war's immutable nature by underlining one of Clausewitz's most significant points, one that is constantly quoted with little willingness to understand its implications. The Prussian theorist notes: "We see, therefore, that war is not merely an act of policy but a true political instrument, a continuation of political intercourse, carried on with other means."[11] Yet, one notes that there are current commentators on terrorism announcing that Clausewitz is no longer relevant in this new age of terrorism. What they miss is that unless one pursues war with a political purpose in mind, one is simply committing murder. For all

---

11. Clausewitz, *On War,* p. 87.

its murderous behavior, ISIS has a political aim, one admittedly
wrapped up in its religious ideology, but a real, palpable political
purpose in terms of its actions.

Unfortunately, the creation and conduct of a clear political
framework that connects means to ends has rarely been a major
attribute of political and military leaders. In his most ironic passage,
Clausewitz notes "[n]o one starts a war—or rather, no one in his
senses ought to do so—without first being clear in his mind what he
intends to achieve by that war and how he plans to conduct it."[12] The
problem throughout the ages has been the fact that war, because it
involves the killing of a large number of one's enemies, invariably
unleashes second- and third-order effects that change the dynamic
of relations between states and nations. Political purposes may drive
nations to war, but in the end there will always be unintended
effects that will directly affect those who have chosen to cross the
divide between peace and war into a conflict they believe will solve
the difficult political problems of today. The most perceptive com-
mentator on human conflict from the sharp end of face-to-face
combat to war's terrible impact on human societies is the ancient
Greek historian Thucydides. His warning is well worth remember-
ing as we move ever deeper into the twenty-first century: "war is a
stern teacher; in depriving them of the power of easily satisfying
their daily wants, it brings most people's minds down to the level
of their actual circumstances."[13]

One might object that this is no longer the case, since the wars
in Afghanistan and Iraq have had so little impact on the United States

---

12. Ibid., p. 579.
13. Thucydides, *History of the Peloponnesian War*, p. 242.

and its citizens with the exception of those who have served in those conflicts. But those wars have been expeditionary wars of choice, conducted far from the shores of North America. And perhaps the wars of choice may affect more than only those who deployed to Afghanistan and Iraq, as the blowback from Western involvement in the Middle East comes ever closer.[14] That said, it is also worth noting that on the ground, the insurgencies that America's invasion of Iraq in 2003 created seem to be becoming ever more violent. Moreover, these conflicts have sparked civil wars with terrible overtones of religious conflict within the Islamic world. Again Thucydides:

> So revolutions broke out in city after city, and in places where the revolution occurred late the knowledge of what had happened previously in other places caused still more extravagances of revolutionary zeal, expressed by an elaboration in the methods of seizing power and by unheard of atrocities in revenge. . . . Fanatical enthusiasm was the mark of a real man. . . . Anyone who held violent opinions could always be trusted and anyone who objected to them could not be trusted.[15]

One of the more interesting aspects of the study of war is the fact that Thucydides' account of the Peloponnesian War and Clausewitz's *On War* retain much of their validity for understanding the problems of human conflict in the twenty-first century. In fact, they remain among the few truly important books about war. The persistence of these works at the top of any serious list of books about

---

14. It would seem that there already has been a blowback from the spreading war in Iraq and Syria in terms of terrorist activity in Europe.

15. Thucydides, *History of the Peloponnesian War*, p. 242.

conflict reflects the fact that their authors intuitively grasped the fact that war is a nonlinear phenomenon. In fact, nonlinearity is the basic framework within which the universe works. As an historian of science, Alan Beyerchen, has noted:

> Nonlinear systems are those that disobey proportionality or additivity. They may exhibit erratic behavior through disproportionately large or disproportionately small outputs, or they may involve "synergistic" interactions in which the whole is not equal to the sum of its parts. . . . Nonlinear phenomena have always abounded in the real world. But often the equations needed to describe the behavior of nonlinear systems are very difficult or impossible to solve analytically. Systems with feedback loops, delays, "trigger effects," and qualitative changes over time produce surprises, often abruptly crossing a threshold into a qualitatively different regime of behavior.[16]

Until the advent of the computer age, the full impact of nonlinearity on the human condition was a matter of conjecture; at best it could only be sensed. And that is why the greatest historian of war, Thucydides, and its greatest theorist, Clausewitz, could not fully lay out the phenomena (human conflict) they were describing. War more than any other human activity engages the senses of those unlucky enough to engage in it. Its attributes consist, among many others, of fear, horror, rage, confusion, pain, helplessness, nauseous anticipation, and at times hyperawareness. It is in these vagaries that

---

16. Alan Beyerchen, "Clausewitz, Nonlinearity, and the Unpredictability of War," *International Security*, vol. 17, no. 3 (Winter 1992–1993), pp. 62–63.

imponderables and miscalculations accumulate to paralyze the minds of military and political leaders. As Clausewitz noted about the conditions of combat, "[I]t is the exceptional [human being] who keeps his powers of quick decision making intact."[17]

Perhaps the most important of war's attributes is friction—those almost infinite number of seemingly insignificant incidents and actions that can go wrong, the impact of chance, and the horrific impression of combat on human perceptions. Clausewitz noted that "everything in war is simple, but the simplest thing is difficult." It is friction that throws sand into the gearbox. "The military machine . . . is basically very simple and therefore easy to manage. But we should bear in mind that none of its components is of one piece: each part is composed of individuals, every one of whom retains his potential of friction." And for anyone who had dealt with substantial numbers of subordinates, Clausewitz's comment that "the least important of whom may chance to delay things or somehow make them go wrong" rings all too true. In the end "friction is the only concept that more or less corresponds to the factors that distinguish real war from war on paper."[18] It inevitably arises "from fundamental aspects of the human condition and unavoidable unpredictabilities that lie at the very core of combat processes."[19] Underlining the capacity "of human errors compounded by 'process and equipment failures'" (frictions) to create disastrous mistakes was the October 3, 2015, attack on the hospital run by Doctors Without Borders hospital in Kunduz, Afghanistan. The C-130 gunship killed 42 in

---

17. Clausewitz, *On War*, p. 115.

18. Clausewitz, *On War*, p. 119.

19. Barry D. Watts, *Clausewitzian Friction and Future War* (Washington, DC, 2004), p. 78.

attacking the hospital which was half-a-mile distant from the target the aircraft was supposed to attack.[20]

Within the innumerable frictions that can thwart, distort, or in some cases even benefit one's conduct of war, chance is clearly at the top of the list. For Clausewitz, "[n]o other human activity is so continuously or universally bound up with chance. And through the element of chance, guesswork and luck come to play a great part in war."[21] For his part, Thucydides consistently uses the word *tyche*—usually translated as "chance," but often left out of translations—which we might translate in a wider sense: things that happened which one had no expectation of happening. Thus, at the opening of the Peloponnesian War, the Thebans had every expectation that their sudden raid on the Athenian ally Plataea would go without a hitch. At its outset everything worked perfectly. No one raised an alarm at the approach of the raiding party of Thebans at dusk; traitors within the city kept the gates open; and the Thebans and their allies seized all the important positions. But then matters went wrong. The relieving main force ran into a major, unexpected spring storm; the rain extinguished its torches; the guides got lost. As the main Theban force floundered across the muddy paths in the mountains leading to Plataea, the locals regained control of the city. Thus, the sudden strike had completely failed, sparking the disastrously long Peloponnesian War.

Adding to such obvious accidents or unexpected occurrences is what military historians have traditionally termed the "fog of war": the inability to see, comprehend, or understand what one cannot

---

20. *The New York Times,* 29 April 2016.
21. Clausewitz, *On War,* p. 85.

perceive in the immediate foreground of one's eyes or ears. It is this constant fog and the accompanying frictions that turn war from the simple into the complex. Perhaps, the clearest way to understand the nature of the "fog of war" is to recognize that it is simply another term for uncertainty. The marine corps' basic manual *Warfighting* describes uncertainty in the following fashion:

> Uncertainty pervades [combat] in the form of unknowns about the enemy, about the environment, and even about the friendly situation. While we [can] try to reduce these unknowns by gathering information, we must understand that we cannot eliminate them—or even come close. The very nature of war makes certainty impossible: all actions in war will be based on incomplete, inaccurate, or even contradictory information.[22]

Clausewitz discusses the inevitable connection of war with human nature in similar terms: "The art of War deals with living and with moral forces. Consequently it cannot obtain the absolute, or certainty; it must always leave a margin for uncertainty, in the greatest things as much as in the smallest."[23]

In combat, commanders and their subordinates make mistakes, either because their assumptions are faulty or because under the pressures of combat they decide on courses of action that make no sense. Chance distorts, disrupts, and confuses those charged with executing the most carefully thought-through plans. Uncertainty and unpredictability dominate the battle space. No amount of computing

---

22. US Marine Corps, *Warfighting*, p. 7.
23. Clausewitz, *On War,* p. 86.

power will eradicate the basic messiness of combat, where fear, terror, and weariness stalk those attempting to make sensible decisions. Where friction prevails, tight tolerances, whether applied to plans, actions, or material factors, inevitably will lead to mistakes and failure.

Adding to the complexities involved in uncertainties is the fact that change is inherent in the very nature of war and its conduct. This is not simply a matter of the fact that our perceptions of the enemy and the choices available to him are never entirely clear, but war is in all respects an emergent phenomenon in many ways similar to biology. The traditional narrative of combat on the Western Front during the First World War is one of the opponents slogging it out from complex trench systems. In fact, in 1914 soldiers had barely scratched out trench lines in the dirt where the opposing armies had come to rest, while by 1918 trenches had almost entirely disappeared, replaced by thin lines of machine gunners in foxholes with the bulk of the infantry far back out of range of the artillery.[24]

Even where adversaries share a similar historical and cultural background, the mere fact of their belligerence guarantees profound differences in attitudes, expectations, and behavioral norms, the American Civil War being a particularly good example. Despite the fact that Americans, Northerners and Southerners, had seen their fate intertwined from the early days of their revolution against the

---

24. For a discussion of the constant changes in weapons systems, tactics, and capabilities and the uncertainties this introduced into the battles on the Western Front, see Williamson Murray, *Military Adaptation in War, for Fear of Change* (Cambridge, 2013), ch. 3.

British, neither side possessed the slightest understanding of the depth of feeling that the war would raise among its opponents. For Southern whites, it was a matter of a few quick thrashings of the Northern "mudsills" (factory workers from the slums), which would quickly convince their opponents to give up and recognize the Confederacy as an independent nation. On the other side of the Mason-Dixon Line, Northerners firmly believed that the great majority of Southern whites, having been manipulated by the radical slaveholders, remained loyal in their hearts to the Union, and one or two quick victories by Union armies would persuade them to return to their allegiance to the United States. Ulysses Grant, the war's greatest general, noted, "Up to the battle of Shiloh, I, as well as thousands of other citizens, believed that the rebellion against the Government would collapse suddenly and soon, if a decisive victory could be gained over its armies."[25] Grant's mind changed after Shiloh, and he was one of the first to recognize that the war would be one long slog. By the time the war was over, the casualty total was well over three-quarters of a million dead in a country of slightly over 30,000,000.[26]

Where different cultures come into conflict, the likelihood that adversaries will act in mutually incomprehensible ways is even more likely. The Asian sage Sun Tzu once noted that "if you know the enemy and know yourself you need not fear the results of a hundred

---

25. Ulysses S. Grant, *The Personal Memoirs of U. S. Grant*, vol. 1 (New York, 1886), p. 368.

26. Demographers examining the Census data in the Southern states from 1870 and 1880 and comparing it to the 1860 Census have calculated that Confederate armies undercounted their losses by as much as 100,000.

battles."[27] The problem, of course, is that rarely, if ever, do political or military leaders have a coherent, accurate understanding of the other, his culture, his history, much less his ability to sustain a conflict. If they did, there would be far fewer wars, but that is precisely the point: they don't. The American record over the past several decades is particularly atrocious. Ignorant of history, foreign cultures, and even foreign languages—13 percent of the CIA's analysts spoke or read a foreign language in 2009—Americans and their military have proven inept over the past half century in understanding their opponents and adapting to the actual conditions they confront. Given the current disarray of American education from grade school through university levels, this is unlikely to change.

What military historians often refer to as the fog of war has its roots in the reality that what occurs on the other side of the hill will always remain opaque, no matter how sophisticated our understanding of the enemy's culture, doctrine, and history. Decision making in war reflects innumerable factors: among others, the competence, or incompetence, of enemy commanders, the capacity of their military forces to display initiative, their understanding, or lack thereof, of our system. The impact of chance occurrences will affect decisions in fashions that we can rarely divine. Clausewitz commented on the reliability of intelligence in forming an accurate picture of the enemy in the following terms:

> By "intelligence" we mean every sort of information about the enemy and his country—the basis in short, of our own plans and operations. If we consider the actual basis of this information,

---

27. Sun Tzu, *The Art of War,* translated by Samuel B. Griffith (Oxford, 1971), p. 84.

how unreliable and transient it is, we soon realize that war is a flimsy structure that can easily collapse and bury us in its ruins. . . . Many intelligence reports in war are contradictory; even more are false, and most are uncertain. . . . This difficulty of *accurate recognition* constitutes one of the most serious sources of friction in war, by making things appear entirely different from what one had expected.[28]

As we suggested above, the sophisticated technological means available to commanders have only served to add a very different friction to the business of understanding the enemy and what he is doing.

The military analyst Barry Watts, himself a product of Andrew Marshall's Office of Net Assessment, has put forth a series of propositions that sum up the realities involved in the fundamental nature of war:

Proposition I: War is a violent two-sided contest of opposing wills dominated by Clausewitzian friction.

Proposition II: Outcomes [in war] are highly contingent, and the various indirect effects or second-order consequences arising from a campaign or war may not be knowable until sometime after the conflict has ended.

Proposition III: In combat, from moment to moment, it is the differential between the levels of general friction experienced by the two sides that matters most.

---

28. Clausewitz, *On War*, p. 117.

Proposition IV: So long as human purposes, frailties, proclivities, and limitations remain an integral part of war, Clausewitzian friction will retain the potential to make the difference between success and failure.[29]

We might end this section with a short discussion of Clausewitz's trinity, perhaps his most important and also his most misunderstood concept. He comments at the end of Book 1 that "as a total phenomenon war's dominant tendencies always make it a remarkable trinity—composed of primordial violence, hatred, and enmity, which are to be regarded as a blind natural force; of the play of chance and probability within which the creative spirit is free to roam; and of its element of subordination, as an instrument of policy, which makes it subject to reason alone." To make his point clear, he then adds that "the first of these three aspects mainly concerns the people; the second the commander and his army; the third the government."[30] Unfortunately, too many facile users of Clausewitz focus on the second description rather than the first.

And it is clearly the first of these descriptions of the trinity on which Clausewitz wants us to focus. In fact, his intention is to describe a nonlinear phenomenon, one that the scientists of his time had come across during this period—namely, if one suspends a pendulum between three magnets of equal size and then releases the pendulum, one can never replicate exactly its previous swings.[31]

---

29. Watts, *Clausewitzian Friction and Future War,* p. 53.

30. Clausewitz, *On War,* p. 89.

31. For a fuller discussion of the relationship between the Clausewitzian triangle and the scientific experiments of the time, see Beyerchen, "Clausewitz, Nonlinearity, and the Unpredictability of War."

Thus, in using the trinity as a metaphor Clausewitz is underlining the fact that these three simple parts of the equation of war will never reoccur in exactly the same fashion. Moreover, if one adds to the difficulty of the problem of war the fact that the enemy will find himself equally affected by his triangle, which will impact his actions and which in turn will interact with our triangle and actions, one gains an insight on why Clausewitz notes that "absolute, so-called mathematical, factors never find a firm basis in military calculations. From the very start there is an interplay of possibilities, probabilities, good luck and bad that weaves its way through the length and breadth of the tapestry."[32]

THE EVER-CHANGING KALEIDOSCOPE OF WAR: THE CHARACTER OF WAR

Change is inherent in everything that has to do with human affairs. It has become an integral part of war as developed in the Western world that was simply not true before the sixteenth century. If war remains a human endeavor, a conflict between two learning and adapting military forces, changes in the political and strategic framework, adaptation by the enemy, and the onward march of technology all have formed and altered its character. Moreover, military leaders find themselves prisoners of their time. As Clausewitz notes each "war and its forms result from ideas, emotions, and conditions prevailing at the time—and to be quite honest we must admit that this was the case even when war assumed its absolute state under

---

32. Clausewitz, *On War*, p. 86.

Bonaparte."[33] Unfortunately, in considering the war that confronts them and driven by an inherent desire to bring order to the disorderly processes of politics and war, human beings tend to frame their thoughts about the future in terms of continuities and extrapolations about the present and only occasionally about the past. Thus, they tend to confuse what is fundamental to the nature of war and the particular characteristics of *their* war.

The course of the American military over the past three decades underlines the extent of the changes that have occurred over that period. In October 1983, when the Grenada operation that overthrew the Cuban-sponsored New Jewel movement occurred, jointness was a concept more honored in its breach than its observance. In terms of capabilities, stealth did not exist outside of the research and development communities. The M1 tank and the Bradley fighting vehicle were only starting to reach the army's forward-deployed units in Germany. GPS did not exist. The training ranges of the National Training Center, Twentynine Palms, Fallon, and Nellis had just begun to change US preparations for war. And finally precision attack was largely a matter for tactical nuclear weapons.

We need to understand the factors that have in the past and will continue in the future to alter the character of war. A paper delivered at the spring 1991 meeting of the Society for Military History suggested that Western military institutions since the fourteenth century have confronted periods of massive change. Such periods have been followed by ones of relative calm during which armies and navies, and later air forces, had adapted to these major changes

---

33. Ibid., p. 580.

in their environment, a pattern biologists have called "punctuated equilibrium." Such a framework offers a path to understanding revolutionary change in the character of warfare as well as providing a perspective to understand better what is happening in our own era. Divided into relatively small nation-states with few geographic features to protect them (the exception being of course England), the political states of Western and Central Europe found themselves in an intensely competitive atmosphere that pushed them to adapt or face annihilation. It also pushed their military institutions to innovate in new and novel ways not only in the realm of tactics and operations, but also in technology and logistics. Those who innovated and adapted survived, and more often than not prospered. Those who failed to innovate and adapt in terms of both their military organizations and their economies fell be the wayside with at times disastrous results for their population. Not surprisingly, Europe's military organization proved skillful at adapting to the innovations and improvements that their opponents had created.

There was, moreover, in the period beginning in the early seventeenth century an historical pattern.[34] Two phenomena were present. The first involved massive change in the political, social, and military landscape within which states have operated. We might term these "military-social revolutions." The second phenomenon led to the creation of major military changes in tactics and operational concepts, both usually but not always influenced by changes in

---

34. Much of the following discussion rests on an article I wrote in *Joint Forces Quarterly* and which was subsequently refined by myself and Professor MacGregor Knox in the opening chapter, "Thinking about Revolutions in Warfare," in MacGregor Knox and Williamson Murray, eds., *The Dynamics of Military Revolution, 1300–2050* (Cambridge, 2002).

technology and the political framework. It also resulted in organizational and administrative innovations that supported or enabled the conduct of war. We might term these phenomena as "revolutions in military affairs." One historian characterized the former as earthquakes and the latter as the preshocks and aftershocks that accompanied the great "military-social revolutions" in the human landscape.

The defining feature of the "military-social revolutions" is that they have fundamentally altered the framework within which wars have occurred. One might characterize the five major "military-social revolutions" in the following terms:

1. The appearance in the late seventeenth century of the modern nation-state, which created and rested on the organization of large disciplined military forces, responsive to the central authority.

2. The French Revolution of the late eighteenth century, which enabled the French state to mobilize the full potential of its population and the nation's resources to meet the threat posed by the invasion of the *ancien régime* powers.

3. The Industrial Revolution, which began in the mid-to-late eighteenth century in Britain and which allowed the British to deploy their great navy which controlled the seas around Europe as well as the world's oceans, support a major army on the Iberian Peninsula, and provide the financial backing for the great coalitions which eventually brought Napoleon down in the great campaigns of 1813 and 1814.

4. The American Civil War and the First World War, which combined the legacies of the French and Industrial Revolutions and set the pattern for twentieth-century war.

5. The advent of nuclear weapons which, contrary to all
precedents, prevented the Cold War from becoming hot
in the decisive European and Northeast Asian theaters of
political confrontation.

"Military-social revolutions" recast societies and states as well as
their military forces. And their effects are cumulative. States that have
missed the earlier "military-social revolutions" cannot easily leap-
frog to success in war by adopting the trappings of Western military
technology. Oil brought Saddam Hussein massive quantities of Soviet
and French hardware. But weapons alone cannot confer battlefield
effectiveness on forces conscripted from a society that lacked an
effective state structure, nor the solidarity and resilience to over-
come the deep clefts between Sunni and Shi'a and Arab and Kurd,
nor the technological skill common throughout societies that have
passed through the Industrial Revolution.

The first of the five great military revolutions introduced a degree
of order and predictability into the conduct of war that since the
collapse of the Roman military system in the fifth century AD had
largely been the province of anarchic improvisation. In the Middle
Ages and the early modern period, governments had with few
exceptions exercised only the loosest of control over their fleets and
armies. When sovereigns called up armies, their first move was to
move their soldiers to someone else's territory since they could
neither pay nor feed them. With pay more often than not in arrears,
the armies pillaged. In 1576, the unpaid soldiers of the Spanish
monarchy mutinied and sacked the great trading city of Antwerp—
an action that wrecked Spanish political aims in the Netherlands and
advanced the cause of the rebellious Dutch. That mutiny reflected

both the inherent indiscipline of the soldiers and the inability of the Spanish state to compensate them in spite of the immense quantities of gold and silver pouring in from Spain's possessions in the New World. Similar episodes of armies mutinying occurred throughout the Thirty Years' War in the seventeenth century, a war that devastated Germany and Central Europe and led to a massive collapse in the population of those areas.

But beginning in the first decades of the seventeenth century, some forward-looking thinkers began the processes of turning armed mobs into disciplined, well-trained armies. The Swedish Articles of War of 1632 made clear that soldiers would dig when they were told to dig, an uncommon occurrence in the days since the Roman legions. Impersonal military discipline made the military organizations of Europe in the mid-to-late seventeenth century and their soldiers and sailors infinitely more effective than the mercenary companies, hastily recruited locals, and sailors off merchant vessels that they replaced. The new military instruments were self-reinforcing; they backed up with force the collection of taxes needed to pay the troops regularly. In return for pay and sustenance, the state could demand that its soldiers maintain a disciplined obedience in garrison as well as on the battlefield. One might note of particular importance was the speed with which the European powers and their military organizations copied and adapted to the improvements and innovations that their enemies made in tactics, technology, engineering, and organization.

The French Revolution further widened and deepened the state's grip on its wealth and the manpower of its citizens. It represented the second great "military-social revolution." The secular ideology of equality and nationalism injected into war a ferocity that matched the religious fanaticism of the previous century, at least for a short period. In 1793, faced with a foreign invasion that they had unleashed themselves through their nationalist lunacy, the leaders of the French Republic declared a *levée en masse* that placed the French people and their possessions at the disposal of the state for the duration of the war. The result was that the French tripled the size of their army in less than a year, and while their forces remained tactically inferior to the armies of the *ancien régime*, they absorbed casualties at a rate that none of the enemies of France could match.

Clausewitz best caught the impact of the French Revolution's massive mobilization of men and resources:

> Suddenly war again became the business of the people—a people of thirty millions, all of whom considered themselves to be citizens. . . . The people became a participant in war; instead of governments and armies as heretofore, the full weight of the nation was thrown into the balance. The resources and efforts now available for use surpassed all conventional limits; nothing now inhibited the vigor with which war could be waged, and consequently the opponents of France faced the utmost peril.[35]

French conquest and tyranny ultimately forced upon the other peoples of Europe a willingness to meet the French on their terms, but only after a series of catastrophic defeats in Central Europe, the most famous of which were Ulm (1805), Austerlitz (1805), Jena-Auerstedt (1806), and Friedland (1807). As Clausewitz points out,

---

35. Clausewitz, *On War,* p. 9.

it would take the *ancien régimes* twenty years to understand the nature of the war they confronted against the French. The combatants of the American Civil War and the two world wars would later replicate with even greater ruthlessness and effectiveness the social and political mobilization that the revolutionaries in Paris had initially pioneered.

Nearly concurrently with the French Revolution, the first stages of the Industrial Revolution were already underway in Britain. Although its impact took longer to affect the military balance, one might consider it the third "military-social revolution" to reverberate through the Western world. The upheaval changed radically the economic underpinnings of British society and placed unimagined resources in the hands of the nation's leaders. Yet, at least over the course of the French Revolutionary and Napoleonic Wars, the Industrial Revolution offered no immediate tactical advantages on the battlefield.

But it did allow the British to contribute to France's defeat in three major ways. First, the massive mobilization of Britain's civil and naval strength allowed the British to dominate the global oceanic commons, control the world's trade, and impose an effective blockade on France and its allies when it served their purposes. Second, the British were able to project their power onto the Iberian Peninsula where they supported Spanish armies and guerrillas in a murderous struggle that Napoleon accurately characterized as his "Spanish ulcer." Along with that effort they supported the Duke of Wellington's increasingly effective military forces in Portugal and then into Spain. Britain's final, and perhaps its most important, contribution came with the financial support it provided to its allies in Central and Eastern Europe. Only that financial support allowed the Russians, Prussians, and Austrians to mobilize their population and resources sufficiently to overwhelm Napoleon in the great campaigns of 1813 and 1814.

The Crimean War of 1853–1856 was the first conflict that saw the Industrial Revolution directly impact the conduct of operations on the battlefield with the introduction of rifled muskets and the movement and support of Anglo-French forces to the Crimea by steamship. But the opposing powers (the British and French on one side, the Russians on the other) were unwilling to mobilize their populace; thus, in every respect the conflict remained limited in scope. The American Civil War was another matter. Both sides followed the path of the French Revolution in mobilizing mass armies. From a federal army of approximately 17,000 officers and men, the Union had mobilized 1,000,000 men by 1864, 600,000 of whom were in the field fighting the Confederates.[36] But it was the combination of the Industrial Revolution with its steadily increasing industrial power and the mass mobilization of its manpower that allowed the North to project its military forces over continental distance and directly into the South's heartland. That deadly combination eventually allowed the Union to crush white Southern resistance and terminate the Confederacy's existence.

The most apparent "revolution in military affairs" came with the North's employment of railroads and steamships to deploy its massive armies across continental distances. The logistical infrastructure for that war-winning effort had to support the Union effort against Atlanta in 1864, from the factories in New England and New York

---

36. For a discussion of the marriage of the French and Industrial Revolutions, see the introduction to Williamson Murray and Wayne Hsieh, *A Savage War: A Military History of the Civil War* (Princeton, NJ, 2016).

to Cairo, Illinois, and from there through Nashville and Chattanooga all the way to Atlanta. It represented a logistical effort that dwarfed that of Prussia's use of railroads in the German Wars of Unification. Thus, the American Civil War represented the fourth great "military-social revolution" in the Western way of war. It foreshadowed World War I and its marriage of the Industrial and French Revolutions. For those who fought in the American Civil War, the result was a frighteningly lethal conflict that in the end destroyed the antebellum White South as a society. The "bummers" of William T. Sherman's army, who turned the towns of Georgia and South Carolina into "Chimneyvilles," were the grim precursors of Bomber Command's "dehousing" of Germany's population.

Concurrently with the American Civil War, the Europeans fought three major wars, but all of them escaped the terrible confluence of the Industrial and French Revolutions. However, the Franco-Prussian War came perilously close to replicating what had happened in North America. With the onset of the war against France, the Prussian chancellor, Otto von Bismarck, unleashed the rabid dogs of German nationalism, largely for internal political reasons, to insure the creation of a unified German state. Not surprisingly the French replied in kind.

What kept matters from exploding into a war of nations was the fact that Napoleon III and his generals proved extraordinarily incompetent—to such an extent that during the conflict's opening phases they managed to maneuver nearly the whole of France's professional army into disastrous defeats at the end of which the French armies surrendered at Metz and Sedan. The disastrous defeats prevented the leaders of the Third Republic, Napoleon III's successors, from replicating the *levée en masse* of 1792. The cadres necessary to train the new armies of the Third Republic were moldering in Prusso-German prisoner of war camps.

Not until 1914 did the Europeans experience the full ferocity of the fourth "military-social revolution." The political results of the First World War would not finally be settled until the fall of the Berlin Wall in 1989, followed shortly thereafter by the collapse of the Communist empire. The "revolutions in military affairs" over the course of the First World War were equally groundbreaking. The tactical problems created by the enormous changes in technology and the inventions of the Industrial Revolution were immense and explain the stalemate that resulted far better than the supposed stupidity of the generals. The internal combustion engine, the products of modern chemistry which ranged from smokeless powder to gasoline, modern rifled weaponry, aircraft, not to mention barbed wire—these inventions, created largely for peacetime purposes, when put in the service of combat operations, provided a nightmare to those charged with "winning" on the modern battlefields of the First World War. The problem for those engaged in attempting to solve the conundrums raised by modern weaponry was that they faced a kaleidoscope of choices. The answers lay in how military organizations could fit the pieces together. Moreover, their opponents were at the same time engaged in processes that rearranged the pieces on the battlefield. Thus, there were no simple or obvious answers to the murderous slaughter on the battlefields of the First World War.

The armies that fought across the Western Front from 1914 to 1918 in effect invented combined-arms warfare. A British or German brigade commander from 1918 would have been able to understand much of what was happening in the Gulf War of 1991, once he understood the greater speed and capabilities of the forces that the coalition deployed. A regimental commander from 1914, however, would have been able to understand virtually nothing about the tactical deployment of forces in three dimensions. Likewise, the navies of World War I explored war in three dimensions and three elements. They pioneered submarine warfare, carrier operations, and amphibious warfare. In the air, the opposing air services made use of the aircraft in every role, except airborne operations, that would appear in more effective form in the following global struggle. The First World War was to be followed by an even more devastating war which involved the fourth "military-social revolution" on an even greater scale and which came close to destroying many of the world's major cities.

The development and then use of nuclear weapons during the period of 1941 to 1945 constituted the most recent of the "military-social revolutions." Its employment against the Japanese cities of Hiroshima and Nagasaki forced an unwilling Japanese military to recognize the obvious and prevented a catastrophic military campaign. But its greatest impact was that of Sherlock Holmes' "dog that did not bark in the night." The accumulation of armaments, quite accurately characterized as weapons of mass destruction, held the ideologically driven superpowers from engaging in a Third World War. Whether an unwillingness to use such weapons in the future, as they slowly proliferate, will remain one of the great moral and strategic questions that will confront the political and military leaders in the twenty-first century.

As suggested above, these great "military-social revolutions" have spawned "revolutions in military affairs" that reflect the times, technology, and inventiveness of those within military organizations and their societies. These lesser transformations do appear susceptible to human direction, and in fostering them, military institutions that possess a questioning and open culture can gain a significant advantage. Military organizations and their leaders embark on "revolutions in military affairs" by devising new ways of organizing and financing themselves or new concepts to destroy their opponents more effectively. To do so they must come to grips with fundamental changes in the social, political, and military landscape; in some cases they must anticipate those changes. "Revolutions in military affairs" require the assembly of a complex mix of tactical, organizational, doctrinal, and technological innovations in order to implement a new conceptual approach to warfare or to a specialized sub-branch of warfare.

The linkages between past "revolutions in military affairs" and the great "military-social revolutions" are sketched out in the table below, although not all of the "revolutions in military affairs" are included. In considering them there are a number of salient characteristics. First, even during great conflicts, they take a considerable period of time to develop. It took the armies of the Western Front four long years to develop combined arms tactics. In peacetime, given the limitations of funding and the constraints of not being able to fully replicate combat conditions, "revolutions in military affairs" take even longer to reach fruition and then have to be refined in combat.

If adapting to wartime conditions is extraordinarily difficult, those involved in peacetime innovation confront almost insoluble problems; it is here that the leaders of military institutions earn their pay. The historical record of the twentieth century suggests that

Table of RMAs associated with military-social revolutions

Military-Social Revolution No. 1: *the seventeenth-century creation of the modern state*

Associated and resulting RMAs:
— Dutch and Swedish tactical reforms, French tactical and organizational reforms, creation of naval power with oceanic reach
— Creation of war offices and admiralties, Britain's financial revolution in financing war

Military-Social Revolution No. 2: *the French Revolution*

Associated and resulting RMAs:
— National political and economic mobilization; wars of battlefield annihilation
— Immense implications for warfare in the future; wars now a matter of national will

Military-Revolution No. 3: *the Industrial Revolution*

Associated and resulting RMAs:
— Provided Britain with immense economic power to fight global naval war, support war on the Iberian Peninsula, and support allies on the Continent

Military-Social Revolution No. 4: *Combination of Industrial and French Revolutions: American Civil War and World War I*
— Provided Union and Confederacy with popular support to wage the Civil War
— Provided North with logistical ability to project military power over *continental* distances
— Changed the tactical balance in favor of the defense
— World War I increased the staying power of military and national entities to an even greater degree
— Invention of combined-arms tactics
— Arrival of war in the third dimension
— Formed basis for innovations during the interwar period and the adaptations in the next conflict

Military-Social Revolution No. 5: *the nuclear revolution*
— Ended the Pacific War between Japan and the United States without the disastrous consequences a continuation of the war would have caused
— Most likely prevented a massive military confrontation between the United States and the Soviet Union

many have not. As a retired army general noted in summarizing the lessons suggested by an examination of a series of case studies on the effectiveness of military institutions in the first half of the past century:

> [I]n the spheres of operations and tactics, where military compe-tence would seem to be the nation's rightful due, the twenty-one [case studies] suggest for the most part less than general profes-sional military competence and sometime abysmal incompetence. One can doubt whether any other profession in these seven nations during the same periods would have received such poor ratings by similarly competent outside observers.[37]

Yet, military institutions do confront immense obstacles to inno-vation in peacetime. Michael Howard has compared their problems to those confronting a surgeon who must prepare to operate with-out the benefit of experience on live patients. Armies, navies, and air forces must train and organize their forces to function on short notice in extraordinarily dangerous circumstances that by defini-tion cannot be replicated in peacetime training. Moreover, they often lack the lavish financial and staunch political support needed for realistic peacetime experimentation and training. And to cap it all, often they do not know when, against whom, and in what political circumstances they will find themselves committing their forces.

---

37. Lieutenant General John H. Cushman, "Challenge and Response at the Operational and Tactical Levels," in Allan R. Millett and Williamson Murray, eds., *Military Effectiveness,* vol. 3, *World War II* (London, 1988), p. 322.

What made the adaptations to the conditions of combat so difficult in the First World War was the fact that a whole host of technological innovations had occurred in the long peacetime period before the outbreak of hostilities in August 1914. A significant number of those innovations had occurred in the civilian sectors, but they disrupted military operations in a completely unexpected fashion and with devastating effects that proved so difficult to unravel that it took Europe's military organizations four years of slaughter to develop tactical answers that worked. The invention of barbed wire to fence cattle and horses in represents a particularly good example of simple advances in the civilian sector that raised nightmarish problems for those trying to break through enemy defensive lines on the Western Front. Used in huge quantities on the Western Front, it made offensive movement even at the tactical level enormously difficult for the attacking Allied armies.

THE SIXTH MILITARY-SOCIAL REVOLUTION: COMPUTERS, COMMUNICATIONS, AND SOCIAL MEDIA

It has also become clear that at present the world is in the midst of as great a "military-social revolution" as any that have come before. And unlike the massive changes that occurred from 1914 to 1990, developments and innovations in the external world are driving much of that change. Significantly, the patterns that characterized the past century have shifted. As we pointed out above, the period before the First World War saw vast technological, social, and economic scientific and technological developments which were so wide in

scope and vast in their implications that it took military organizations
four long, blood-soaked years before they had the glimmerings of
what combined arms would involve.

But over the course of the next seven decades, military organizations took the lead in pushing the boundaries of technology and
technological innovation. Their impact on the Second World War
would lead to an even greater slaughter, this one involving civilians
as well as those involved on the sharp end of combat. Nevertheless,
the technological and electronic innovations and adaptations would
eventually prove to be of immense value to the civilian world. In
fact, by 1945 they had changed the nature of travel and communications. The most obvious example would come in terms of aircraft
design and capabilities. The aircraft of 1919 had little real applica-
tion in the civilian world, but those of 1945, within a matter of a
decade, had created the possibility of air travel that reached well
beyond the imagination of most experts several decades earlier.
Thus, the technological and scientific developments of the Second
World War had an immense impact on the economies and technology of the civilian world.

Not surprisingly, the same was to be true in the period of the Cold
War, at least outside of the Soviet-Communist bloc. The United
States embarked on the space race with the Soviet Union in the late
1950s and early 1960s for purely military reasons. The unintended
spin-offs from that race, however, were to have an immense impact
on the civilian economy, particularly in the long-term development
of communications and on computer-assisted devices. Simple hand-
held telephones now possess access to processing power that dwarfs
the computer power of all the world's computers in the 1960s. Yet,

the road to the current explosion in information devices was never smooth. The air force almost killed off GPS in the 1980s, while George H. Bush released the Internet from the control of DARPA and defense department almost as an afterthought. Certainly, few in the early 1990s had a clue about the unintended effect it would have not only on human interactions but global commerce as well.

That said, it is also worth noting that the baby has escaped its controllers. Since the end of the Cold War, it has been in the civilian sector that the "military-social revolution" has been picking up speed. If this revolution is on the magnitude of the previous revolutions of this sort, then the resulting uncontrollable onrush of events has enormous implications for the use and the effectiveness of military forces. How it will impact the use of military forces, however, remains shrouded in the highest security classifications as well as the uncertainties of how opposing forces will interact in combat. But the combat implications may well be only a part of the problem. The rapid dissemination of information, not to mention pictures, through the Internet and the 24/7 media have already underlined the problems that the conduct of military operations will confront.

The problem today, as in 1914, is that the full implications of the use of modern technology in a contest between equally sophisticated opposing sides remain unclear and uncertain. Moreover, as one of the most sophisticated military thinkers in the United States, Colonel Richard Sinnreich, USA (ret.), once observed to this author, the greatest problems that US military organizations may confront will come when enemy actions severely degrade US communications, computers, and technical devices through cyber and other forms of attack. The American military undoubtedly will be doing the same to its opponents. Thus, the side that "wins" may well be the side that has best prepared to operate in the dark.

Whatever the possibilities, the world is in the sixth of its great "military-social revolutions" and the implications for military forces remain far from clear. The crucial determinant will be how quickly and flexibly US military forces and their commanders adapt to the actual conditions that they confront. Adding to the complexity of the problem is the fact that the onrush of technological change does not rest only on the expenditure of massive resources; in some cases it provides America's opponents with dangerous possibilities that rest on their ability to harness the brainpower of their followers.

The "military-social revolution" is here, but modern commentators and so-called military experts should be warned against believing that they can comprehend its full extent or its long-range implications. In particular, it will not end the all-encompassing influence of friction on the employment of military force. One might close the discussion in this chapter with another quote from military analyst Watts which underlines the danger of the persistent belief that the increasingly sophisticated computer power and sensors will allow modern military forces to significantly mitigate the influences of what Clausewitz so accurately termed friction:

> Consider, after all, how much would have to be overturned or rejected to conclude [that friction will not remain a major factor in the conduct of war]. Among other things, one would have to overthrow nonlinear dynamics, the second law of thermo

dynamics, the fundamental tenets of neo-Darwinian evolution-
ary biology, and all the limiting metatheorems of mathematical
logic, including the famous incompleteness theorems by Kurt
Gödel and the extension of Gödel's work by Gregory Chaitin to
demonstrate the existence of randomness in arithmetic. No
small task indeed![38]

---

38. Watts, *Clausewitzian Friction*, p. 84. Clausewitz notes that in calculating
all the factors that politicians and generals should consider, "to master all this
complex mass by sheer methodical examination is obviously impossible.
Bonaparte was quite right when he said that Newton himself would quail before
the algebraic problems it would pose." Clausewitz, *On War*, p. 586.

3

THE NEMESIS OF HUMAN AFFAIRS: THE EVER-CHANGING LANDSCAPE

Ministers and policy advisers never see clearly the effect that their decisions have in the theater of operations. But in war more than elsewhere, purpose and means exist in permanent reciprocal relationship. However valid it is for political intentions to give events their initial direction, the means—that is, fighting—can never be regarded as an inanimate instrument. Out of the rich vitality of war grow a thousand new motives, which may become more significant and dominant than the original political considerations.

Clausewitz, *On War*

IF THE CHARACTER OF WAR HAS UNDERGONE SIGNIFICANT CHANGES over the centuries, the same is true to an even greater extent with the strategic and economic landscape on which men have interacted. Given the relatively short life of human beings in comparison to the span of history, it is difficult for most, including those at the pinnacle of power, to grasp the rapidity with which change occurs even in the present. The young, of course, have no direct knowledge of the past; their lives exist almost entirely in the present; they can remember the past only in terms of the few years they have lived. Most of those few interested in the past, academic historians and social scientists, rarely take stock of the rapidity and depth of change in human affairs, because they have lived in the comfortable safe havens of universities and colleges, while the rest of humanity simply ignores the past.

Thus, only a few great statesmen and historians have any sense of the fact that they are riding a world awash in change, the second- and third-order effects of which they can barely sense. It is the fact that radical and unforeseen change—the "black swans of history," to use a modern term, events that cannot be predicted—is so fundamental an aspect of the world in which we live that attempts to predict the future accurately founder in a morass of the unexpected. Bismarck once described the role of the statesman in the following terms: "In politics you cannot focus on a long-range plan and proceed blindly in accord with it. All you can do is draw the broad outlines of the directions you seek to follow."[1]

The previous chapter suggested the extent to which change has altered the capabilities of America's military since 1983.[2] The same has been true in terms of the technological landscape. In 1983, the Internet existed only in the department of defense and a few academic institutions; virtually no one saw the communications revolution coming, much less the economic possibilities that it would

---

1. Quoted in Marcus Jones, "Strategy as Character: Bismarck and the Prusso-German Question, 1862–1878," in Williamson Murray, Richard Hart Sinnreich, and James Lacey, eds., *The Shaping of Grand Strategy, Policy, Diplomacy, and War* (Cambridge, 2011), p. 86.

2. A meeting of computer experts in the late 1970s, as the possibility of personal computers was emerging, could only imagine their use as making shopping lists.

offer. Cellular phones did not exist. Personal computers were beginning to come into widespread use, but their reliability was depressingly inadequate. Microsoft was beginning to emerge from Bill Gates's garage, while Google existed only in the imaginings of science fiction writers and a few perceptive scientists. In other words, the revolution in information and communications technologies, taken for granted today, was largely unimaginable in 1983. The revolution had begun, but few saw its implications.[3]

In 2008 my colleague James Lacey and I, writing the 2008 *Joint Operating Environment* for Joint Forces Command and General Mattis, set out a chart of the strategic balance over successive decades to emphasize the extent that change has dominated the history of the past century. Both of us, serious students of history, nevertheless, found the chart astonishing in the extent of the changes that had occurred decade by decade in the twentieth century. It is useful to revisit a slightly reworked version of that chart.

1900   *If you had been a strategic analyst of the world's leading power, you would have been British, suspiciously evaluating the policies of France and Russia.*

1910   *You would now be allied with France, and Germany would represent a serious threat.*

1920   *Britain and its allies had won the First World War, but the war had seriously harmed Britain's financial position, while the possibility of a naval race loomed with both the United States and Japan.*

---

3. One might similarly note that few commentators today have grasped the implications of autonomous robots.

1930   For the British, the naval limitation treaties were now in place, the Great Depression had begun, and defense spending for the next five years would assume the "ten-year rule"—no war would be possible for at least a decade. British planners posited the main threats to their empire as the Soviet Union and Japan, while Germany and Italy were either friendly or represented no threat.

1935   A British planner would now posit three great threats: Italy, Japan, and, worst of all, a resurgent Germany.

1940   The collapse of France in May and June left Britain seemingly alone, confronted by Germany's undefeated Wehrmacht with a Japanese threat looming in the Pacific. The Soviet Union was fulfilling the Reich's orders for raw materials with great eagerness, while a desperate United States was attempting to begin a massive attempt to make good its military deficiencies.

1950   The British were no longer a great power. The atomic age had begun, a Cold War between the United States, now the world's greatest power, and the Soviet Union. The Americans suddenly found themselves drawn into a "police action" in June that would kill more than 35,000 Americans, nearly 58,000 South Koreans, and nearly 3,000 Allied soldiers, and leave nearly 2,000,000 Korean civilians dead. The Chinese represented the main enemy for US forces in the Korean War.

1960   The Cold War continued with both the Soviets and the Americans expanding their stockpiles of nuclear weapons. In American strategy, massive retaliation would soon give way to flexible responses, while a small insurgency in South Vietnam hardly drew American attention. Average time an average S&P company could expect to remain on that business benchmark was sixty-one years.

1970   *The United States was beginning to withdraw from Vietnam, its military forces in shambles. The Soviet Union had just crushed an incipient Czech political rebellion in the Warsaw Pact. Détente between the Soviets and Americans had begun, while the Chinese were waiting in the wings to create an informal alliance with the United States.*

1980   *The Soviets had just invaded Afghanistan, while a theocratic revolution had overthrown the shah's regime in Iran, the kingpin of America's strategy in the Persian Gulf. "Desert One"—an attempt to free American hostages in Iran—ended with a humiliating failure, another indication of what pundits were calling America's military forces: "the hollow force."*

1990   *The Soviet Union collapses. The supposedly hollow force shreds the supposedly "battle-hardened" Iraqi Army in less than a hundred hours. The United States has become the world's greatest debtor nation. No one outside the department of defense and academia was using the Internet, while The World Wide Web lies in the world of science fiction.*[4]

2000   *Warsaw is the capital of a North Atlantic Treaty Organization nation. Terrorism is emerging as the greatest threat to the United States. Globalization has reached a level of percentage of gross global product that it had reached before the First World War. Biotechnology, robotics, nanotechnology, HD energy, and so on, are advancing so fast that they are beyond forecasting.*

2010   *The United States has withdrawn entirely from Iraq and will soon begin withdrawing from Afghanistan, two wars that cost the*

---

4. By 1994 that would radically change, with some 17,000,000 users in the United States alone.

Americans nearly a trillion dollars. The Middle East is in a
shambles, while a small group of fanatical Muslims will soon
emerge in Syria to threaten retribution on the Western world as
what it believes will be the first step to re-creating the caliphate of
the eighth century. The average life span of an S&P 500 company
is now approximately twenty years.

The possibility of future troubles in a world of massive change, in spite of the claims of American political scientists, seems entirely likely, especially given the increasing lack of economic and political control that the United States has been able to exercise over the past decade. Moreover, in contrast to the two decades that followed the collapse of the Soviet Union, there are currently serious military challenges to America's continued dominance, with China and Russia being the foremost threats. In fact, the current strategic environment may be the most unstable and dangerous the United States has faced since the late 1940s, with the Soviet explosion of an atomic bomb and an American military, weakened by the massive demobilization that took place after World War II, confronting Soviet conventional strength in Central Europe. The difference, of course, is that in 1949–50, the United States faced one great threat, namely the Soviet Union, while at present, America's military planners confront a multiplicity of threats, all to an extent uncertain but all with the potential to destabilize the global balance of power. Such threats obviously exist between nation-states, but one should not ignore the disturbing economic and political trends, especially a strong current of isolationism within the United States as well. In the long run, some may represent existential threats to the security and lives of Americans, and others may not. The complex difficulty that US leaders will face will lie in understanding which of those represent major threats and which are simply nuisances on the international scene.

Whatever threats emerge over the period of the coming decades, they are going to require strategic wisdom from America's political and military leaders as well as the ability to adapt their political and military assumptions to a world that is undergoing rapid and incalculable change. In an essay written in 1990, Paul Kennedy underlined the extent of the problem that confronted British military planners between 1930 and 1935:

> At the beginning of the 1930s, [British planners] regarded the Soviet Union as the greatest land enemy of the Empire, while in naval terms the chief rivals were the United States and Japan; they saw Mussolini's Italy as temperamental, France as unduly assertive and difficult (but not hostile), and Germany as still prostate. Five . . . years later, Japan appeared as a distinct challenge to British interests in the Far East, Germany had fallen under Nazi rule and was assessed as the greatest "long-term danger," and Italy's policies appeared aggressive and hostile, whereas the United States was more unpredictable and isolationist than ever, Russia had become somewhat less of a direct strategic threat (but remained an ideological foe), and France's weaknesses were more manifest than its strength.[5]

The international world of radical strategic change in the character of the threats facing British military planners is a world that

---

5. Paul Kennedy, "British 'Net Assessment' and the Coming of the Second World War," in Williamson Murray and Allan R. Millett, *Calculations and the Coming of World War II* (New York, 1992), p. 35.

has considerable similarity to what the United States and its leaders will confront in the coming decades of the twenty-first century, a world that will ultimately demand rapid adaptation to the unexpected.

THE LOOMING BLACK SWANS

It is not difficult to imagine potential disasters—some natural, some manmade—that could wreck the framework on which the current global political and economic base rests. The most obvious case would be a meltdown of the global economy, which would have consequences far beyond its economic impact. The second- and third-order effects in economic terms are obvious: spiraling unemployment rates, plunging stock markets, governments desperate to find the financial means to meet their obligations. But the consequences would have results far beyond the economic spheres.

The Great Depression provides some clear indications as to what one might expect to happen to the relationships among the major powers. Within a year of the Wall Street crash in October 1929 and the collapse of the global economy, the Japanese Army, seeking to provide Japan with an escape from the rapid decline in that nation's European and American markets, launched an invasion of Manchuria that began the disastrous conflict with China, which would destabilize East Asia over the course of three decades. In Europe the German election of September 1930 moved Hitler's National Socialist group of extremists from a small, seemingly insignificant party to the largest party in the *Reichstag*. In just over two years,

Hitler would become the Reich's chancellor and the course leading to the Second World War would begin to unwind. German rearmament would begin within a matter of days of Hitler's entering into political power on January 30, 1933.

On the other side of the ocean, in 1935 the United States found itself so overwhelmed by its economic and political difficulties that its president and Congress attempted to fence the nation and its economic and political strength off entirely from the happenings in the rest of the world with the Neutrality Acts, which forbade the export of US arms to any nation that was involved in war. Meanwhile, the European democratic powers, misled by the idle belief that no major power would engage in a major war again, minimized their armament programs in spite of the rising specter of German rearmament.[6]

Clearly the Great Depression ended any chance of a return to the globalized economy of 1913 for another half a century. It may well have had a greater impact in causing the Second World War than the strategic effect of the Great War itself. The economic impact of the Depression splintered the thin bonds of cooperation among the democratic powers, each of which turned inward to handle the second- and third-order effects of a collapsing economic and political world. In spite of the increasing belligerence of Japan, Italy, and, most threateningly of all, a rapidly rearming Germany, the democratic powers of France, Britain, and the United States

---

6. Adam Tooze's brilliant book *The Wages of Destruction: The Making and Breaking of the Nazi Economy* (New York, 2008) spells out the major economic difficulties the Germans had throughout the prewar period.

continued to minimize defense expenditures until quite literally the last moment.[7]

In the case of the United States, the expansion of its ground forces, which ranked in size with those of Bolivia's in the interwar period, would not begin until the summer of 1940, when the collapse of the French state finally underlined to the American polity how dangerous the international environment had become. Until that point most Americans had remained with their heads firmly buried in the sand, while even those like their president, Franklin Roosevelt, who recognized the growing danger of the rapidly rearming Germans and Japanese, believed that the United States could confine its effort to air and naval forces and the nation's productive capabilities.

It is, of course, impossible to predict the impact of any sustained economic meltdown of the world economy sometime in the near future. And such a collapse will not necessarily follow the path of the Great Depression in the early 1930s. But similar patterns would undoubtedly arise. For some political entities, new radical leaders would arise and preach aggressive policies aimed at both internal and external enemies. The 1930s certainly suggest that might be the case, while the current popularity of demagogues such as the French Marine Le Pen and the American Donald Trump suggest that such a phenomenon is already occurring. Other nations will cut back on

---

7. Ironically true of the French who elected a popular front government of socialists and communists with the result that French rearmament stagnated in the key period from 1936 to 1938. In Britain, the Chamberlain government allocated only minimal resources to the military until March 1939 so that the British could have supplied only two ill-equipped divisions to the Continent had war broken out in fall 1938 over the Czech crisis.

their participation in international affairs; virtually all will cut their foreign aid budgets, if they have any, as they grapple with increasingly severe internal problems.

For those with any kind of representative government, it is highly likely that, just as in the 1930s, they will slash their defense budgets to the bone to meet their financial obligations to their citizens. Authoritarian governments that pay little or no attention to popular attitudes will increase defense spending, in some cases to maintain order among their own population and in some cases to encroach on their neighbors' territory against whom they have irredentist claims—sometimes justified, in most cases not—as the basis of their actions.[8] During the past half century the United States and its military forces have exercised considerable influence in retarding such conflicts through the global presence of American military power, which has generally exercised a retarding effect on the risk takers.[9]

Beyond the possibility of an economic catastrophe that wrecks the global economy lie further destabilizing possibilities. Some undoubtedly will appear bizarre, at least until they occur. These range from natural disasters; others could involve the man-made possibilities of miscalculations leading to a conflict between major powers that might spiral out of control into the use of nuclear weapons. There is also the possibility that national leaders will risk

---

8. The Russians have already moved in this direction with the weak states in Central Asia, with their large populations of ethnic Russians being an inviting target.

9. In the late 1960s at the height of tension between the Soviet Union and Communist China, the Soviets intimated to the Americans that they were thinking seriously of taking out China's nuclear capabilities. Would the United States take advantage of such a situation, the Soviets inquired? The response was yes. The Soviet attack never took place.

aggressive war rather than face internal political challenges. On the side of natural disasters that have a real potential for causing immense dislocations, perhaps the least likely, but the one that would cause the most damage to the global infrastructure, would be a massive solar flare such as the one which occurred in 1859 and was of sufficient strength to disrupt much of the world's telegraph systems. A 2012 study of the impact of a similar solar flare striking the Earth suggested that the resulting damage would range between $0.6 trillion and $2.6 trillion in knocking out much of the global infrastructure of computers and communications.

There are obvious economic and international trouble spots, such as the Middle East, that underline the dangerous world we live in and the considerable potential for mankind to move to its dark side—namely, the penchant for human beings to turn to war as an easy solution to whatever their current difficulties might be or what the negative consequences might be. The chapter will now turn to some of the most obvious, with the understanding that there is every possibility that there are other possibilities that could threaten the international equilibrium.

THE ECONOMIC CLIFFS

Overall, the period since the Second World War has seen an order of magnitude growth in the economies of the Western world that has carried over into the economies of East Asia and eventually into

I am indebted to James Lacey, my colleague and friend, for helping me put together this short section on the increasingly dangerous global economic situation.

that of China. There have been ups and downs. But even with the huge defense expenditures the Cold War required, the West and, slowly, other areas of the globe have enjoyed an extraordinary period of economic growth, now more than seven decades long. But while economic growth has spread to outliers like India and significant parts of Africa, serious tremors have threatened the global economic structure during the past several decades. This study does not aim to examine the economics of human conflict or its direct contribution to the outbreak of wars, past, present, or future. But some examination of the potential for a general systemic collapse of the current economic order is necessary to understand whether the possibilities of major wars or simply the continued litany of small-scale conflicts will continue to disturb the planet.

In the mid-1980s the flow of funds sloshing around the world's financial markets each day was on the order of several hundred million dollars, a figure that the major central and trading banks could handle, even given the primitive nature of the computers they were using. By 2008 that number had expanded to more than a trillion dollars, a flow that was reaching beyond human grasp. The ability of several currency traders to lose a billion dollars in trades only covers over by their exorbitant losses the innumerable other multimillion-dollar trades that have gone south over the past several decades. The point here is that to a considerable extent the financial markets have expanded beyond human control.

Whether computers can make up for human failings or will exponentially compound them remains open to doubt, but what is certain is that central banks and various national monitoring agencies like the Securities and Exchange Commission confront the challenge in trying to catch dangerous trends before they boil over into catastrophe. The wonderful film *The Big Short* catches the disinclination of the supposed police of the security markets such as Moody's and Standard & Poor's to do anything more than join the herd of lemmings in their rush over the cliff into the financial disaster of 2008. Nothing in their performance suggests that they will act any more critically, decisively, or altruistically in the future.[10]

Beyond the possibility of a meltdown of the global financial markets, one of the most worrisome trends has been the steady ratcheting up of the US debt, which has reached $20 trillion. That total would still be manageable except that politicians on both sides of the aisle in Congress are unwilling to take any substantive actions to either reduce expenditures or increase revenues. The most important would have to be a willingness to cut back on the swelling tide of entitlements, but other painful medicine would clearly involve increased taxes and decreases in government services. But the willingness to cut back on entitlements represents the most important medicine. Certainly defense funding represents another real possibility to cut the need to borrow and that is already happening. Unfortunately for the United States, the current political climate of irrelevance suggests that Congress will refuse to take the necessary medicine. Thus, default will be the most probable outcome. Whether the default takes place as a catastrophic collapse (Greece), a ruinous hyperinflation (Weimar Germany), or a default of promised entitlements, the results will be unpleasant in political terms, threatening perhaps the very fabric of the Republic.

---

10. The movie is based on Michael Lewis's book, *The Big Short: Inside the Doomsday Machine* (New York, 2011).

The results of such an economic breakdown would also have a calamitous impact on defense spending and the capabilities of US forces to operate in an effective fashion. General Mattis commented to the author at the height of the 2008 economic meltdown that the pundits in Washington, instead of arguing over whether the US Navy should have ten or eleven carriers, should be thinking about how the United States would deploy four carriers, if four were all the nation could afford. And there is no democratic state with the capabilities or willingness to step in to take the place of the United States and its military forces.[11]

One is reminded of the hard choice that the Athenian people had to make in 483 BC. In that year, Athenian miners discovered a massive seam of silver in the mines at Laurium. The choice was whether to employ this windfall in building up the Athenian Navy with a substantial number of triremes or to disburse the silver among the Athenian citizenry. At the time the Persian threat seemed far away, although that was to change in the next year, when the Persians would begin preparations for launching their great invasion of Greece. Nevertheless, despite the apparent ambiguity of the Persian threat, the Athenian assembly—led by the greatest of all Athenian politicians, Themistocles—voted to use that silver to build 200 triremes, which would play *the* decisive role in the victory of the Greeks over the Persians at Salamis in 480 BC.

---

11. Presently the Chinese People's Liberation Army has neither the capabilities nor the interest in participating in a major fashion in policing the global commons. In fact it appears more interested in disturbing the current equilibrium, especially in Southeast Asia.

But it is clear that that decision in democratic Athens only came as a result of Themistocles's brilliant political leadership. In opposition was a considerable body of the citizenry who much preferred to enjoy the immediate gratification of silver deposited in their hands instead of having the polis spend it on the building of warships to protect Athens against a distant, far away threat about which they knew little. In the end, Themistocles won the argument, but only after extraordinary political efforts. Whether the American people and their representatives would display strategic wisdom in similar circumstances is very much open to doubt.

Even the assumption that the debt load is manageable, at least for the present, does not mean that it is not having negative effects. For instance, though the extent to which national debt loads are already crowding out more productive investment is not quantifiable with any certainty, the effect is certainly considerable. Moreover, the pressures of governmental debt load are happening on a global scale, as the requirement to roll over old debt is crowding out commercial borrowers, even as new state debt threatens the solvency of many nations. Despite the rise in debt levels, bringing with them the threat of multiple state bankruptcies, the slow rate of growth around the globe is still encouraging many nations to continue borrowing.

In any case, the political environment in the United States is making it difficult, if not impossible, to fund a new spurt in Keynesian spending. The global economy may well have hit a Keynesian limit, where current state debt loads make additional deficit spending impossibly dangerous. John Maynard Keynes's proposals made sense when he first promulgated them in the 1930s, a time when most states were desperately attempting to remain within balanced budgets, except, of course, Nazi Germany with its massive outlays on defense spending. Ironically, Germany's enormous spending on defense in the prewar period came close to bankrupting the nation and played a significant role in Hitler's decision to invade Poland in September 1939 and start the Second World War.[12]

For the past several years, as fiscal initiatives have become increasingly constrained, central banks have stepped in to prop up their national economies. Through extraordinary measures, global central bankers have kept interest rates at an unnaturally low level—even testing the market's appetite for negative rates—by pumping cash into the system. While one can make an argument that such coordinated actions by the central banks have managed to stave off financial and economic disaster, such efforts have not succeeded in pulling the global economy out of its doldrums. Moreover, the central bankers will not be able to extend such actions indefinitely into the future, and the time is coming when central bankers are going to have to throw in the towel. The inevitable rise in interest rates that will follow will make even current national debt loads unsustainable, much less those that come into existence several years down the road.

In addition, over the past four decades a series of financial crises have seriously damaged both the regional and global economies. Several of these for a time threatened to tip over into what could have approached a worldwide depression. Two crises in the 1980s, the Latin American debt crisis of 1982 and the American savings and loan crisis of 1986, remained largely localized in their impact. The Asian crisis of 1997 was more serious in its global impact. Circumstances came close to triggering a "perfect storm" of financial and

---

12. For the major economic difficulties that Germany faced in the prewar period, see Tooze, *The Wages of Destruction*.

economic turbulence. As a result of excessive and poorly supervised borrowing, fixed exchange rates, and large current-account deficits, many Asian countries were beset by speculative attacks. As currencies collapsed under the strain, companies found it impossible to make payments on their dollar-dominated debts. The result was another bout of capital flight from the countries affected to the United States and other safe havens that exacerbated debt payment difficulties with a dire impact on more than a billion human beings.

The Asian collapse spread to Russia and came close to seizing up the global financial system when the hedge fund Long-Term Capital Management (LTCM) took a major hit on its Russian-linked investments. LTCM's exposure in Russia cost it nearly $2 billion in just a few weeks, and the fund was on the verge of collapse. At the time there was widespread fear that the firm's collapse would cause a chain reaction of failures across the financial community. When LTCM could not raise additional capital on its own, the Federal Reserve stepped in and organized a nearly $4 billion bailout. Ironically, Bear Stearns and Lehman Brothers refused to participate in the bailout; not surprisingly, both firms found themselves friendless when they required capital injection in 2008. There is no reason to go into detail about the 2008 collapse, by far the worst of the major financial crises of the past four decades, since the readers of this work all remember how close the global economy came to a general collapse on the order of what happened in 1929.

For the present, the longer national leaders postpone the debt reckoning, the greater the likelihood that the reckoning will be catastrophic. A global meltdown would be the worst of all scenarios. As one nation after another defaults, while simultaneously vacating its entitlement pledges, the stress on internal as well as international relations and domestic stability would increase by an order of magnitude. Perhaps even more dangerous for the international environment would be the fallout when politicians, struggling for personal survival, pursue dangerously chauvinistic policies. In many cases the political results of a sense of disenfranchisement and abandonment would lead to the replacement of democratic regimes with authoritarian regimes of the far left and the far right, a pattern which will resemble that of the 1930s with inestimable negative consequences for peace and stability throughout the world. In what direction such regimes would go in terms of their foreign policies and how aggressive they might be is indeed unpredictable. Nevertheless, one is reminded of Churchill's great words that in such a case the world might "sink into the abyss of a new Dark Age made more sinister, and perhaps more protracted, by the lights of perverted science."[13]

THE PROBLEM OF FAILED STATES

Over the past several decades, political scientists have spent considerable time in examining the problem of failing states. The 2008 *Joint Operating Environment* examined what the authors regarded as a far greater problem, namely, that of failed states. In particular they singled out Mexico and Pakistan as possibilities. In the case of the former, Mexico's proximity to the United States carried with it the specter of the immense damage that a Mexican collapse into anarchy would entail, as well as the threat of mass migration from the south. The

13. Churchill's comments came in his speech in June 1940 immediately after the fall of France. Quoted in James C. Humes, *Churchill: The Prophetic Statesman* (Washington, DC, 2012), p. 80.

threat that Pakistan carried was that of the problem of what would happen to its nuclear weapons, should it collapse. But in 2008 only Somalia and the nuisance caused by its pirates represented an actual failed state.[14]

Since 2008, a number of new failed states have joined the ranks of Somalia. Located in the Middle East and among the Arab world, they carry with them a significant threat to the balance of the whole region and perhaps to the world's oil supplies. The collapse of Iraq and Libya were the direct result of reckless and feckless policies executed by the Bush and Obama administrations; Syria's collapse came as the United States and the European powers stood by and watched the situation spin out of control. Yemen joined the wretched ranks of failed states as a result of the machinations of the Saudis and the Iranians. In every case, these external interventions have resulted in the slaughter of tens of thousands with totals that appear to have every prospect of growing. The collapse of these states has already involved civil, tribal, and religious fighting, with every possibility that their troubles will expand beyond their territories.

The most significant of these cases has been the collapse of Iraq as a result of the inexcusable incompetence of the initial American occupation. President George W. Bush and his closest advisers allowed a Sunni insurgency to explode from 2003 through 2006, an explosion that soon led to the inclusion of the Shi'a. Ironically, after the coalition had dampened the fires of religious and political conflict with the surge of US forces in 2007–8, the new American

---

14. The failed states in Africa such as Sierra Leon represented a threat only to its neighbors rather than to the international community.

ambassador, Christopher Hill, who knew nothing about the area and who refused to listen to those who did, proceeded to wreck what chance there was of a settlement with the support of a president who cared only about leaving Iraq as fast as possible whatever the damage might be. Thus, the US troops were gone by early 2011, and Iraq's Shi'a regime, with now only Iranian influence in Baghdad, followed a course of radical policies that thoroughly antagonized the Sunnis. The sudden arrival of ISIS in northern Iraq was a direct result.

But the Western ability to make astonishing policy decisions that paid no attention to the potential disastrous effects did not end at that point. The Arab Spring brought with it widespread political uprisings. In both Libya and Syria those uprisings quickly morphed into outright civil war. In the case of the former, Moammar Gadhafi and his regime quickly collapsed with the Western powers and the United States providing a considerable nudge with air and missile support for the rebels. But no support for the rebels appeared on the ground, as if the Americans and Europeans were incapable of learning the most obvious lessons from the previous decade about what happens when state-backed military and police disappear from the scene. The uprising in Libya indeed overthrew Gadhafi with American and European help. But what replaced his regime was internecine tribal strife, murderous gangs, and general chaos, an ideal breeding ground for the dark movements crawling in the gutters of the Islamic world.

How exactly the resulting mess will sort itself out is impossible to predict, except that those responsible, the Europeans and the Americans, seem unwilling to intervene to restore some minimal form of political order. The American government and its ambassador in Libya immediately displayed their lack of understanding of a situation marked by violence by neglecting to provide sufficient security to protect the embassy. The removal of state power, no matter how corrupt, in the Second and Third Worlds does not necessarily result in its replacement by another form of state power, as occurred in the Russian Revolution of 1917. Rather it results in a political vacuum in which local ethnic and religious groups, long impoverished and mistreated by dictatorial regimes, take over and provide an ideal climate for extrastate and transnational actors to plow the soil. In the short term, as we have been seeing in Somalia but now spreading to other parts of the Middle East, the result has been civil and religious war, which invariably has the potential to spread beyond local borders.[15]

The situation in Syria has resulted in even greater troubles. The Ba'athist dictatorship of Bashar al-Assad refused to collapse as outsiders so confidently predicted. Instead, it hung on for dear life, undoubtedly due to the murderous end of Gadhafi and his followers. But the regime also proved incapable of putting down the troublesome rising of Sunnis and reformists. Rather than the hoped-for democratic government, what has emerged has been a mixture of murderous competing groups as described by one expert who has spent extensive time on the scene:

> There are those fighting for themselves and their competitive "state-building" projects, including the Kurdish People's Defense Units and ISIS. There are those fighting for the regime of Bashar

---

15. In the case of Somalia, the troubles have spread into the Indian Ocean with widespread piracy along with large refugee camps in Kenya, which provide the breeding grounds for terrorists to threaten that state.

al-Assad including Iran's Revolutionary Guards Corps and an
ever expanding circle of multinational proxies such as Lebanese
Hezbollah; the Fatemiyoun Division of Afghan refugees as young
as 12 year-olds who have been conscripted in Iran to fight in
Syria; the National Defense Force, a super-militia of Shia and
Alawite fighters; three Iraqi Shia militias, the Badr Corps, League
of the Righteous and Hezbollah Brigades. . . . Finally, there are
those fighting for the overthrow of the regime . . . and a host of
Islamist or Salafist brigades.[16]

The appearance of Syria as a failed state does have the potential
for a number of worst-case scenarios. The troubles in Syria have
clearly spilled over to exacerbate the deep-seated divisions in Iraq.
Here the collapse of the state structure carries with it the danger
that the troubles will spread throughout the world's great oil-rich
region. The reckless American invasion of Iraq and the hurried,
feckless departure have fed the century-long divisions within the
Islamic world between Shi'a and Sunni.[17] Nevertheless, one should
not forget that the British cobbled Iraq together from three totally
disparate provinces of the collapsed Ottoman Empire, none of
which possessed close cultural or political affinity, except that they
lived in the same area.

The continued fracturing of the area that formed these two states
into a religious-civil war could spread throughout much of the

---

16. Michael Weiss, "The Syrian Ceasefire Is a Sham," *Daily Beast*, 12 February
2016.

17. For the appalling decisions made by the Obama administration in its exit
strategy from Iraq, see Emma Sky, *The Unraveling: High Hopes and Missed Opportunities in Iraq* (New Haven, 2015).

region. In perhaps his sharpest passage on the implication of such wars in both his own time as well as in the future, Thucydides warned, "then, with the ordinary conventions of civilized life thrown into confusion, human nature, always ready to offend even when laws exist, showed itself proudly in its true colors, as something incapable of controlling passion, insubordinate to the idea of justice, the enemy of anything superior to itself; for, if it had not been for the pernicious power of envy, men would not have so exalted vengeance above innocence and profit above justice."[18]

THE TERRIFYING IMPONDERABLES OF THE FUTURE

It is indeed easy to draw up terrifying scenarios. The problem is that none of them are likely. Nevertheless, given the fact that strategic decision making throughout history has rested on "security, honor, and self-interest," it is entirely certain that war will remain a significant option for those who confront an uncertain and possibly dark future. Moreover, individuals will make the crucial decisions that lead to war. In some cases they will make their decisions wisely, but more often than not such critical decisions will occur as the result of faulty assumptions, thoughtless anger, a general lack of understanding of the opponent, sheer arrogance and ambition, and a belief that war offers an easy and controllable solution to domestic political troubles.

---

18. Thucydides, *History of the Peloponnesian War*, p. 245.

Simply put, human perceptions and judgments are more often than not flawed. In most cases in history, those at the highest levels, politicians as well as military leaders, have proven inept, if not downright incompetent. It is likely that their future imitators, believing themselves to be great statesmen or military leaders, will accept similar comfortable assumptions and believe that they will gain significant advantages from launching into conflict rather than choosing the uncomfortable and difficult other paths, which, among other things, would suggest that war might not represent the best of all choices.

The problem for Americans in the present in attempting to think about the possibilities of war is that they have no real way of estimating the context within which a future war or wars will occur. When Clausewitz was at the *Kriegsakademie,* he received a request to evaluate an exercise for general staff officers of a potential war with Prussia on one side and Austria and Saxony on the other. Outside the military forces available on both sides, the exercise took into its design no mention of the political aims of the opposing governments or of the international situation. Clausewitz was direct in his reply: "There can be no question of a purely military evaluation of a great strategic issue, or of a purely military scheme to solve it."[19]

In other words without an understanding of their political, strategic, and international context, a discussion of military operations has no basis in anything resembling reality, because the political and strategic framework will inevitably, for better or worse, determine and guide the military choices. And that is one reason why military

---

19. Paret, *Clausewitz and the State,* p. 380.

plans, except to establish the logistical parameters and possibilities, are largely irrelevant.[20] But it applies equally to those who are thinking about the strategic future. The political and strategic context within which future wars might occur is entirely opaque. As St. Paul noted, we do indeed see through a glass darkly.

---

20. That is not to suggest that when the logistical parameters have been established that military planners play the slightest attention to the fact that their plans could well fail given logistical gaps. For a particularly egregious case of this, see the discussion of logistical planning for Operation Barbarossa in Horst Boog, *Das Deutsche Reich und der Zweite Weltkrieg,* vol. 4, *Der Angriff auf die Sowjetunion* (Stuttgart, 1983), pp. 248–72.

4

DÉJÀ VU ALL OVER AGAIN

A far more serious menace is the retinue of jargon, technicalities, and meta-phors that attend these systems. They swarm everywhere—a lawless rabble of camp followers. . . . Thus it has come about that our theoretical and criti-cal literature, instead of giving plain, straightforward arguments in which the author at least always knows what he is saying and the reader what he is reading, is crammed with jargon, ending at obscure crossroads.

Clausewitz, *On War*

THE PAST HALF CENTURY HAS NOT BEEN ONE OF THE BRIGHTER passages of time in the history of this American Republic. There was, of course, the victory in the Cold War. But that victory was largely the result of a bizarre Soviet economic system—admired by all too many Western intellectuals—the massive overspending by the Sovi-ets on military hardware, and an aggressive foreign policy that added economic gems such as Cuba, Somalia, Ethiopia, Angola, Mozam-bique, and Nicaragua to Moscow's sphere of influence. But the Vietnam War, the Carter presidency, and the post–Cold War period hardly suggest a high level of American strategic competence, while the capacity of the US military to adapt to unexpected military challenges has not always been impressive. Because of where we stand in the present, the past is crucial to understanding many of the possibilities that lie in wait in the future, as well as for any examination of the course of American strategy and military performance in the future.

Sometime during his epic career as a baseball player and philosopher, Yogi Berra commented about a particular incident in a play that day that it was "déjà vu all over again." For an historian, that epigraph all too aptly sums up the strategic policies of the United States toward what has happened in the past five decades. The Iraq and Afghanistan wars represent in so many ways an echo of the past mistakes and errors America's politicians, military, and bureaucracy have made. The past half century has been a history of strategic decision making based on facile assumptions, in which policymakers and military leaders have been largely ignorant of the language and culture of the nation's enemies and contemptuous of the past, our own as well as that of others. Moreover, our experiences in Iraq closely echoed the British experience in Mesopotamia in 1920. In the 2011 winter trimester at the Naval War College, my students were astonished to discover in reading British Lieutenant General Aylmer Haldane's account of the 1920 uprising in Mesopotamia that the American occupation of Iraq in 2003 had repeated innumerable mistakes that the British had made 83 years earlier in many of the same places.[1]

Thucydides, that greatest of all historians, commented about his writing of his history of the Peloponnesian War that "it will be

---

1. One of the students could not only identify several locations in the photographs in Aylmer Haldane's memoirs, but also the nature of the tribes that the British general describes.

enough for me . . . if these words of mine are judged useful by those who want to understand clearly the events that happened in the past and which (human nature being what it is) will at some time or other and in much the same ways be repeated in the future."[2] And that, of course, is the value of history: to alert the leaders of the present to the dangers that have occurred in the past. Yet tragically that has not been the case among America's policymakers and senior military leaders over the past several decades. Like so many of their fellow countrymen, they ignored everything that even the recent past suggested, much less what history might have warned. Instead they substituted dubious assumptions and theories in place of a comprehensive examination of the past.

If the British experiences in Iraq in 1920 seem too far distant from twenty-first-century strategy and policy, one might have thought that the American experiences in fighting an insurgency in Vietnam in the 1960s would have been of some relevance. In May 1975, the end of the Vietnam War had come as North Vietnamese tanks battered their way into the presidential palace, thus ending the sorry story of America's effort to bring democracy to that portion of Southeast Asia. That attempt had begun in 1954 as American political and military advisers attempted to establish a semblance of a friendly government in the wreckage left by the disastrous French defeat at Dien Bien Phu.[3] The Americans focused their effort to build a democratic, anti-communist state on Ngo Dinh Diem, who had been educated in the United States and who appeared to possess the requisite credentials

---

2. Thucydides, *History of the Peloponnesian War*, p. 48.

3. Bernard Fall's account of the fall of Dien Bien Phu remains the most gripping account of that battle. See Bernard Fall, *Hell in a Very Small Place: The Siege of Dien Bien Phu* (New York, 1966).

and political savvy to establish a government where little existed.[4] And so the United States embarked on a course that would lead to the dark Vietnam Memorial with hardly any in-depth strategic analyses at the various road marks along the way of the costs that might occur, should the United States up its stakes.

Diem was a failure, at least from the American point of view. He and his brothers placed their own political survival above the war on the Viet Cong—at least from the perspective of their American advisers in the field. In particular, the brothers worried that competent, ambitious generals might launch a coup that would overthrow their shaky regime. They were right, at least about the ambitious generals. Shortly before the assassination of President John F. Kennedy in 1963, the generals struck, admittedly with support from the CIA. They not only removed the Diems from power, but executed them as well. However, to the surprise of the supposed American experts, most of whom spoke little French and less Vietnamese, the generals proved even more inept than the Diem brothers.

Thus, throughout 1964 into 1965 the situation steadily unraveled as the Viet Cong and their North Vietnamese supporters ripped the South Vietnamese military to shreds. Unwilling to accept the possibility that South Vietnam might fall, President Lyndon Johnson, Defense Secretary Robert McNamara, and their advisers committed American troops to a desperate military situation. Their military advisers in Washington provided considerable support for the decision to intervene—after all how could pajama-clothed, ill-trained guerrillas stand up against the overwhelming capabilities possessed

---

4. For an account of that effort, see David Halberstam, *The Making of a Quagmire: America and Vietnam During the Kennedy Era* (New York, 2007).

by the United States? From the beginning, America's political leaders and their military advisers deceived the American people about their intentions, capabilities, and prospects, which the title of Lieutenant General H.R. McMaster's book masterfully sums up: *Dereliction of Duty: Lyndon Johnson, Robert McNamara, the Joint Chiefs of Staff, and the Lies that Led to Vietnam.*

The Americans, of course, could have examined the French experiences in Vietnam to winnow out what not to do. After all, had not the great statesman Otto von Bismarck commented that he preferred to learn from the mistakes of others. In 1964 the French government even sent its after-action report on the causes for the defeat to the Pentagon, when it became apparent that their allies where moving toward a major intervention in the conflict. But the US military had little interest in learning from a war the French had botched. The staff officers in the Pentagon immediately consigned it to the classified archives of the National Defense University where it remained unread, at least by those making policy and military strategy across the Potomac.

The American military of 1965 was indeed superbly trained and prepared to fight a conventional or nuclear war against the Soviets. But US leaders were not prepared to fight a war of insurgency against revolutionaries who had defeated the French, the leader of whom had played a major role in the founding of the French, Chinese, and Vietnamese Communist parties. Ignorant of Vietnamese culture and language, as well as the delicate balance of nationalities in Southeast Asia, the Americans wandered into the Vietnam War prepared to fight the wrong war, which they did with a massive mixture of raw military power and political naïveté. Meanwhile, those in Washington played with bizarrely irrelevant political science theories such as signal sending. The bombing of North Vietnam was bound to fail, because the only thing that might have made it work was a campaign of extermination—a course unacceptable to the American people. And neither Johnson nor McNamara was capable of understanding that it was the North Vietnamese and not the Americans who were capable "of paying any price, bearing any burden."[5]

With neither a political nor a military strategy for winning the war, the Johnson administration drew back after the 1968 Tet Offensive had shocked the American people into a modicum of strategic sense. In 1969 a new administration assumed control of the war with the aim of creating a peace that would leave some semblance of American prestige intact; this involved an effort to put the South Vietnamese army on a more effective combat basis in terms of equipment and training. Unfortunately, it was too late. The three years of General William Westmoreland's leadership had seen the Military Assistance Command, Vietnam (MACV), display little or no interest in emphasizing the preparation of the South Vietnamese army to stand on its own. Now with a new interest in training the South Vietnamese to a higher standard under General Creighton Abrams as commander of MACV, there was insufficient time to repair the years of neglect.

Meanwhile, Johnson, unwilling to admit that he had fired West-moreland, brought the general back home to become the army's chief of staff, where he would provide more of the unimaginative leadership that had marked his time as commander MACV. Under

---

5. President John F. Kennedy used the phrase in his inaugural speech in Washington, D.C., in January 1961.

the leadership of the next president, Richard Nixon, and his chief foreign policy adviser, Henry Kissinger, the period from 1969 to 1972 saw the Americans draw down their forces, while the situation in South Vietnam slowly and steadily improved. Endemic corruption and the less than impressive leadership exhibited by the South Vietnamese president, Nguyen Van Thieu, hardly helped matters. But American diplomats and generals hesitated to interfere in the internal affairs of South Vietnam, although their very presence had that inevitable effect. Nevertheless, with the focus on them, the South Vietnamese military steadily improved. However, under pressure from the anti-war sentiment at home, the United States extracted itself from the war after blunting the North Vietnamese's Easter Offensive of April 1972 and savaging North Vietnam's cities and infra-structure in Linebackers I and II with massive bombing campaigns.

Kissinger and Nixon's rationale appears to have been that a decent interval after withdrawal before the South Vietnamese regime collapsed would salvage American prestige. In retrospect, that approach resulted in tens of thousands of more American as well as innumerable Vietnamese deaths. The collapse of South Vietnam's military and then state came in spring 1975. Two factors explain the sudden South Vietnamese collapse: first, the refusal of the Congress of the United States to live up to the promises the Nixon administration had made to provide continued military equipment, which placed the South Vietnamese in a hopeless position against their opponents. Equally important was Thieu's removal of most of his army's most competent corps and division commanders and their replacement with those loyal to him, most of whom were incompetent. He clearly aimed to ensure that no coup d'état would take place against his regime. In that respect he was certainly successful. He was not going to follow the fate of the Diem brothers.

How much prestige the United States managed to save as the collapse gathered momentum is not difficult to access. The withdrawal was a disgrace. The American ambassador to South Vietnam, Graham Martin, refused to authorize sensible precautions as the North Vietnamese drive picked up speed on its way to Saigon.[6] Simply put, he buried his head in the sand and refused to recognize the desperateness of the situation for fear of damaging South Vietnamese morale. Thus, the pullout of Americans from Saigon was a shambles; among other achievements, it left a South Korean lieutenant general behind. The pictures of American military and diplomats scrambling to escape in helicopters from the embassy rooftop hardly did much for American prestige. Most disgraceful of all, the CIA and State Department did little to help those who had supported the American effort escape. Their bureaucracies were simply incapable of acting. Moreover, the CIA even left behind much of the documentation on its operatives for the North Vietnamese secret police to peruse. What they did with those lists is not hard to imagine.

Many of those Americans who had supported the effort in Southeast Asia had predicted a bloodbath should the United States abandon the South Vietnamese. That, of course, was precisely what happened. In contradiction to the argument that many in the anti-war movement had made that a North Vietnamese victory would bring

---

6. See Frank Snepp, *Decent Interval,* for a clear discussion of the irresponsible actions of America's diplomats and intelligence bureaucrats.

peace and social democracy to Vietnam, the North Vietnamese established "reeducation camps" for tens, if not hundreds, of thousands of South Vietnamese, many of whom perished. Large numbers of Vietnamese of Chinese extraction found themselves pitched into dugouts and rowboats in the South China Sea. As a direct result of the American withdrawal from Southeast Asia, Pol Pot's regime in Cambodia waged a campaign that approached genocide against its own people, a reality that most of America's major newspapers shrilly denied. The final irony was that the North Vietnamese had to bring to an end Pol Pot's Khmer Rouge, supposedly for humanitarian reasons.

In the end the United States escaped the consequences of its ill-conducted expedition to Southeast Asia. Admittedly, tens of thousands of maimed and mentally impaired American veterans remained as a reminder of the war. But with the veterans shuffled off to VA hospitals or the lower classes from whence most of them had come, America's military moved into the future, sure that the country would not repeat the Vietnam War. Its military did repair the catastrophic state in which it had left Vietnam. It turned to the threat at hand, the conventional and nuclear forces that the Soviet Union had arrayed across the world, particularly in Europe, a threat that American strategists and officers understood. Slowly, but steadily, time washed the memories of the Vietnam War out of the officer corps as memories faded and Vietnam veterans retired. New capabilities appeared: a host of weapons systems entered the tables of organization and equipment, each better than the previous ones, while the all-volunteer army evolved into an extraordinarily well-trained force.

The Gulf War of 1991 appeared to put the ghosts of Vietnam to bed. That was at least the conclusion of President George Herbert

Walker Bush. Nevertheless, dangerous trends were occurring within the US military. The sudden and unexpectedly complete victory over Saddam Hussein's Iraqi military gave senior military leaders the impression that there was little the US military could not achieve, given its training, capabilities, and technological sophistication. Slogans such as "information dominance" and "full-spectrum capabilities" sprinkled the literature of military journals with arguments that fog, friction, and uncertainty would soon disappear from the military capabilities of the United States.

Making matters worse, most of the huge system of professional military education ignored history, the study of strategy, and military theory in favor of obtuse and superficial discussions of area studies, international relations, and other topics favored by academics. As for war and the profession of arms, forget it. Moreover, the rejection of the study of insurgencies that had marked the post-Vietnam War period continued, even though the great conventional and nuclear enemy, the Soviet Union, had disappeared. Insightful movies such as *The Battle of Algiers* disappeared from the curricula of staff and war colleges. Even Clausewitz, much less Thucydides, the two most perceptive thinkers on human conflict, were only casually addressed in what was supposed to be the serious study of the military profession and strategy.

9/11 came as a terrible shock to the American people and their military. The response certainly underlined the extraordinary capabilities in conventional warfare that the American military still possessed. The reply to the Taliban regime in Afghanistan's contemptuous dismissal of American demands that it surrender Osama bin Laden was sudden and devastating, but entirely conventional in its articulation. One echo from Vietnam still sounded through American policy making. None of the principals—the president, the vice president, the secretary of defense, and their minions—had the slightest interest in "nation building." Thus, Afghanistan received little attention from those in charge in Washington, while too many senior military leaders found the possibility of taking down Saddam Hussein's murderous regime more intriguing than wrestling with the economic and security problems of an Afghanistan wrecked by thirty years of war.

In retrospect, the operational takedown of the Iraqi military represented a thing of beauty in terms of military art. Two reinforced divisions—one army, one marine—supported by additional British divisions, destroyed Saddam's ground forces in a campaign that lasted a little over a month. But what happened thereafter was a disaster. Donald Rumsfeld, the worst secretary of defense in American history—which is saying a great deal—deliberately sabotaged efforts to prepare for the postconflict phase. But it was not just Rumsfeld who was at fault for the disaster that followed. Most of the senior military leaders, with the possible exception of General Eric Shinseki, paid little or no attention to what was to occur in the aftermath of the destruction of Saddam's regime. Because of fears that Saddam's regime was about to collapse, the carefully worked out plans drawn up by General Tony Zinni, commander of Central Command in the late 1990s, were dismissed by his successor, General Tommy Franks, an arrogant mediocrity. Not until the insurgency had devastated much of Iraq for three years, did the army and marine corps actually begin drawing up a manual for best practices in counterinsurgency.[7] Not surprisingly, the key drivers in

---

7. An effort that was led significantly by two of the smartest and well-read officers this author has ever met: James Mattis and David Petraeus.

this were two of the most imaginative general officers in the two services: Generals David Petraeus and James Mattis.

The result was a series of muddled civilian and military decisions, which led to disastrous consequences. No preparation had been made to impose martial law after the occupation of major Iraqi cities and towns by US forces. When the American military had taken down Manuel Noriega's thuggery in Panama in December 1989, the result had been a massive outbreak of looting. One might have thought that the lesson would have been clear: if the military and police have been removed, widespread looting will inevitably occur in nearly all human societies.[8] But again as in Panama, the American military sat by and watched as the Iraqis looted virtually everything not tied down, including the irreplaceable artifacts of their great archeological museum.

Unfortunately, that was only the beginning. One suspects that President George W. Bush and his advisers replaced Lieutenant General Jay Garner in May as the initial official in charge of reconstruction efforts in Iraq, because of the unfavorable publicity the massive looting was occasioning throughout the media. Garner, a last-minute appointment to the postconflict administration, at least had considerable experience in Iraq, because he had run the relief efforts for the Kurds after the 1991 Gulf War. His replacement, Jerry Bremer, had never run a major operation, had served as a State Department bureaucrat for much of his career, knew little about Iraq or its history, and did not speak Arabic.

---

8. The same thing had occurred in Los Angeles in 1992. When the police commissioner pulled the police out of the downtown areas, massive looting immediately broke out.

It is not entirely clear who made the decision to disband the Iraqi Army and police force, while at the same time carrying out a massive de-Ba'athification program, which basically disenfranchised the entire civil service, including nearly everyone who knew anything about the running of day-to-day affairs in Iraq. There was no discussion of the implication of these major decrees; Bremer arrived, ordered them implemented, and lit the fuse for an insurgency. Bremer's ignorance of Iraqi culture and politics showed most clearly when he ordered his subordinates to refuse to have any dealings with the tribes—exactly the mistake the British had made in 1920. With no real conduit to Iraqi political culture, the Americans watched as the situation in Iraq steadily deteriorated. Only the Kurdish areas remained relatively stable.

In retrospect, perhaps the most astonishing aspect of the early American occupation of Iraq was that the military or civilian leaders paid little attention to reconstituting the Iraqi military and police forces despite the fact that they had ordered the Iraqi Army and police force disbanded. Instead, that task remained at the bottom of military priorities in everything from advisers to basic equipment such as weapons and first-aid kits. Only in June 2004, fifteen months after US forces occupied Iraq, did Lieutenant General David Petraeus find himself appointed to the command of the Multi-National Security Transition Command-Iraq. Reasonable resources eventually began to arrive, but everything had to start from scratch. Thus, the Americans had ignored one of the most fundamental lessons from Vietnam until late in the game: foreign troops cannot win an insurgency; only indigenous troops knowledgeable about their own culture and language could do that.

For much of the remainder of the year after the collapse of Saddam's regime in April 2003, much of the American military and political leadership remained in denial that a major insurgency was brewing throughout Iraq, not only in the Sunni areas, but in the Shi'a areas as well. One senior consultant, a Vietnam veteran with two tours, including one as an adviser, visited Iraq in August 2003 and discovered only three of the senior generals (Mattis, Petraeus, and Buford Blount—all interestingly enough the lead division commanders in the invasion into Iraq) recognized that major trouble was in the offing. The military commander of the occupation in the aftermath, Ricardo Sanchez, a newly promoted lieutenant general, failed completely in dealing with the insurgency. For the most part, he accepted the nonsense coming out of Washington that there was no insurgency, but rather the remnants of Saddam's Ba'athist Party and a bunch of criminal gangs. To make matters worse, Sanchez and Bremer refused to cooperate.

The result almost led to a disastrous defeat for the Americans in April 2004. Two separate events precipitated the crisis. In Fallujah, a mob of Iraqis killed four US contractors who had strayed into the town and then hanged the bodies from a bridge abutment. Washington immediately ordered the marines to launch a major attack on the city despite the warnings of Mattis, now returned to Iraq, as to what might occur. The American offensive plastered the city, caused inevitable civilian casualties, and, with the help of the thoroughly dishonest reporting of Al-Jazeera, convinced much of the world's media, including that of the US, that a horrendous atrocity was occurring. At that point Bush pulled back, which provided al Qaeda and the other fanatics in the town cachet with the Iraqi population with propaganda about their "victory." Ironically, Haldane's memoirs of the 1920 campaign in Iraq had indicated that the locals had seen any pullback from a military operation by the British as a political and military victory. But then why read a memoir of an insurgency written eighty years earlier?

As this political disaster was unfolding in mid-April 2004, up the Euphrates, Bremer closed down the papers run by Muqtada al-Sadr, the Shi'ite religious leader who was deeply hostile to the Americans. The Shi'ite cities along the Euphrates exploded, as Sadr ordered his militia to attack the US supply lines running north from Kuwait along the Euphrates. Sadr's militia came close to breaking the key supply lines from Kuwait that were essential to American forces in the center and north of Iraq. American units scheduled for redeployment back to their home stations had to be stopped in midpoint and were thrown into the fight to reopen the logistical lines.

With insurgencies flaming throughout the Sunni and Shi'a areas, Washington finally reacted. It removed Sanchez and Bremer, while Bush placed General George W. Casey, son of an army major general who had died in a helicopter crash in Vietnam in 1970, in command of US forces. Casey, like Westmoreland, represented a safe replacement, a general who would not make waves. Thoroughly unimaginative, Casey was deeply imbued with the army's culture of conventional war; he had little interest or preparation in terms of his professional military education for the political and cultural demands of a complex, three-cornered insurgency—a four-cornered one, if one included the Iranians. Unwilling to recognize the need for different approaches, Casey hunkered down and made few demands on the Pentagon for increased resources or larger numbers of soldiers or marines.

The situation continued to deteriorate from 2004, when Casey took over, through to summer 2006. Improvised explosive devices, increasingly sophisticated munitions shipped by the Iranians to the Shi'a, and increasing terrorist attacks not only were aimed at the Americans, but also reflected intercommunal strife between Shi'a and Sunni communities, the latter of which was threatening to rip Iraq apart in a major civil war. Like Westmoreland in Vietnam, Casey had no solution but to pile on more firepower and hope for the best. By 2006 events had reached a disastrous impasse. At the start of the year, al Qaeda terrorists blew up the golden dome of the al-Askari mosque, one of the holiest shrines for Shi'ite Muslims. That action vastly increased the level of sectarian violence, which made it even more difficult to bring a reasonable level of discipline and evenhandedness to the Iraqi police and army forces the United States was attempting to create.

But perhaps the most serious mistake the Americans would make that year would be to help push Nouri al-Maliki into the prime minister's position. In retrospect, there were other candidates who would have been better, but to the Americans he appeared capable of reaching out to the Kurds and Sunnis. In fact, he was a narrow-minded Shi'ite who would prove consistently resistant to advice. He possessed the deep paranoia that many Shi'a carry in their historical and religious baggage. Thus he would prove a major hindrance to any effort to reknit Iraq's deeply riven political and religious polity. He would also come to place loyalty to his persona among his military commanders above all their other attributes. Like President Thieu of Vietnam and Saddam, he viewed competent senior officers as direct threats to his continued tenure in office.

The congressional election of 2006 represented a wake-up call for Bush and the Republicans. The president finally acted in a presidential manner. He fired Rumsfeld, admittedly far too late, but better late than never. The new secretary of defense, Robert Gates, represented a significant improvement over his narrow-minded and rigid predecessor. At the same time the president removed Casey from Iraq, but, as Johnson had done with Westmoreland, brought the general back home to be the army's chief of staff, where he would contribute little to that service's refashioning.

Bush showed considerable political courage in overriding his military and political advisers in deciding that a major surge of American forces was necessary to buttress a situation that was spiraling out of control. Not only Casey, but also the new CENTCOM commander, Admiral William "Fox" Fallon, the chairman of the Joint Chiefs of Staff, General Peter Pace, and much of the Washington bureaucracy obdurately opposed the surge. But it was not just Bush's advisers who were causing difficulties. Congress was displaying its usual irresponsibility. While the considerable number of Democrats who opposed the war were not willing to cut off funding as their predecessors had in 1973 for the Vietnamese for fear that they would find themselves blamed for the potential fallout, they were certainly willing to trumpet the impossibility that the "Surge" would improve the situation and to treat Petraeus with extraordinary rudeness.

However, they turned out to be wrong. A combination of favorable circumstances in Iraq occurred to turn the military and political situation around. The appalling behavior of most of al Qaeda's operatives convinced many Sunnis, especially the tribal leaders, that the fanatical outsiders represented a greater threat than the Americans.

In the main Sunni areas to the northwest of Baghdad, effective army and marine commanders welcomed and encouraged the Sunni "Awakening," while Petraeus provided the drive, competence, and leadership to turn the situation around. The general received enormous help from the new American ambassador to Iraq, Ryan Crocker, who had extensive experience in the Middle East and who possessed both linguistic and academic credentials that made him deeply knowledgeable about the culture and history of the Arabs. Moreover, and this proved particularly important, Crocker and Petraeus formed an effective and close bond. In other words, there was a real country team in place running American political and military operations in Iraq.

By the time Barack Obama assumed the presidency of the United States, the surge had largely succeeded. Terrorist incidents had declined drastically. Al Qaeda was on the ropes, and US troop withdrawals were already moving ahead. In retrospect, Obama appears to have been uncomfortable with that very success, since it seemed to invalidate everything he had argued in denouncing the surge and urging the immediate withdrawal of US forces from Iraq. At the end of 2008, Petraeus had moved on to become the CENTCOM commander, while Christopher Hill replaced Crocker in early 2009. That appointment was to prove disastrous in every respect.

Unlike Crocker, Hill was a state department bureaucrat with no experience in the Middle East, did not speak Arabic, and almost immediately made it clear that he had little interest in cooperating with Petraeus's replacement, General Ray Odierno. The general's chief political adviser was Emma Sky, a highly educated Oxford graduate with extensive Middle East experience. Hill had nothing but contempt for her, once referring to her as that "goddam fucking

British spy."[9] The real problem was that Odierno's team understood the Iraqis and their culture and politics far better than Hill did. Dealing with an inferior deck in terms of his knowledge of the situation, he did what all too many bureaucrats do: he ignored the advice and counsel of those better informed.

The endgame waged by the Obama administration in many respects resembled that of Nixon and Kissinger in 1972. The difference, of course, is that in the Hanoi Peace Accords, the Americans had to pull all of their military forces out of South Vietnam. In Iraq, there was considerable room to negotiate a final status of forces agreement so that when the Americans withdrew their last combat units, a sufficiently strong US military presence could maintain a reasonable level of training for the Iraqi military and provide a backup should the Iraqis run into difficulties. But the Obama administration began negotiating a status of forces agreement late in the game, so late in fact that one can make the case that it had no intention of leaving any Americans in Iraq at all. In the rush to meet the deadline, Obama and Maliki found it impossible to create a new status of forces agreement necessary to keep the Americans in Iraq. Thus, the Americans left.

Those who had dealt with Maliki in the past had considerable doubts about the prime minister's competence as well as his willingness to work with others than the Shi'a. Not exactly trustful of the Kurds, he clearly regarded the Sunnis as completely untrustworthy. In March 2009, the Iraqis had held another national election. By the time the ballots were in, it was apparent that there was no clear

9. Quoted in Michael R. Gordon and General Bernard E. Trainor, *The Endgame: The Inside Story of the Struggle for Iraq, From George W. Bush to Barack Obama* (New York, 2012).

winner. Nevertheless, Ayad Allawi, a moderate, highly intelligent politician, possessed the largest bloc in the new parliament. There would obviously be considerable political haggling, but had the Americans thrown their weight behind Allawi, he would probably have succeeded Maliki as prime minister. But Hill argued that since much of Allawi's support came from the Sunnis, he should not receive American support.

In fact, the writing was on the wall as to what kind of regime Maliki would run should he receive another term. His thugs were already arresting and torturing Sunnis, while he was pursuing Kurdish and Sunni politicians whom he described as unreconstructed Ba'athists, which amounted to just about anyone he regarded as an enemy. A number of these had been important tribal members in the "Awakening," which had broken al Qaeda. Obama did make an effort to secure the presidency of Iraq for Allawi, but the Kurds, who possessed that position, were not about to abandon the presidency. Maliki, with the Americans' blessing, continued on as before.

Once the Americans were gone, Maliki proceeded on a predictable course of removing the Sunnis by any and all means. Furthermore, he stiffed the Kurds by cutting them off from much of the oil money they were supposed to receive from the Iraqi state. Rapidly, whatever chance there might have been to reach an accommodation among the Shi'as, Sunnis, and Kurds collapsed. But most disastrous for continued peace in the Middle East, Maliki, much like Thieu in Vietnam, removed most of the competent Iraqi generals and senior officers. He replaced them with political appointees with little military competence, interested only in enriching themselves at the expense of the Iraqi state. Training and discipline collapsed, the results displayed most clearly in the defeats of the Iraqi military forces around Mosul against a bunch of hardly well-trained ISIS operatives.

The moral and human results of the failure of American politicians and military leaders to recognize the implications of the past are already apparent. The bureaucracy of the US government has already managed to sabotage congressional efforts to allow many Iraqis who support US efforts during the war to immigrate to the United States. The savage atrocities perpetrated by the ISIS successors to al Qaeda will undoubtedly be paid in full by the Shi'a fanatics on the other side. The bloodbath has already begun. When it will end no one knows.

And so we are left with the dismal possibility that, along with the collapse of the Syrian and Iraqi states, we could see a massive civil war similar to Europe's religious wars of the sixteenth and seventeenth centuries. And at what cost in blood and treasure have the American people paid for their willful ignorance of the past? It is almost tragedy as comedy. One cannot forget the words of Peter Cook, the British comic, at the end of one of his skits: "I have gone over my mistakes from every point of view and am fully confident that I can repeat every one of them."[10] The tragedy of Americans is that we have not bothered even to study our mistakes.

10. Based on this author's recollection having heard the skit on three different occasions.

5

THE AMERICAN PROBLEM

The Greeks, generally speaking, were endowed with spiritual force that allowed them to avoid self-deception.

Simone Weil

In the fighting, they thought it more honorable to stand their ground and suffer death than to give in and save their lives. So they fled from the reproaches of men, abiding with life and limb the brunt of battle; and in a small moment of time, the climax of their lives, a culmination of glory, not of fear, were swept away from us.

Thucydides

As the United States and its armed services approach the third decade of the twenty-first century, they confront a number of challenges. Perhaps the most important are going to involve the difficulties in choosing whether to employ military forces or not. But equally important is the fact that once the decision to go to war has occurred, as Clausewitz suggests, the political and military leadership must understand the character of the war upon which they are embarking and not mistake it for something that it is not. Above all they must have a clear and realistic conception of what they hope to achieve in the conduct of military operations.

Given the extent of the challenges that confront any attempt to maintain stability in a world beset by the actions of fractious humans and their aggressive leaders, no American intelligence organization or political leader will be able to predict the where, the how, the when, the political and military context, or the potential costs of a future conflict involving the United States. Moreover, US leaders must learn to think about the second- and third-order effects that might unhinge their political and strategic plans or which might result from an unwillingness to take action. That ability to prepare for the vagaries of chance must rest on a willingness to challenge the basic political and military assumptions on which policy rests.

Inherent in future American strategic decision making about the use and the utility of military force will be the tension in the division of responsibilities between the political and military leaders. That tension has existed throughout America's wars, perhaps the most egregious being that between Abraham Lincoln and George McClellan, the first commander of the Army of the Potomac. But exacerbating that tension is the likelihood that, in setting the goals for the use of force, the future political leaders of the United States will in most cases be ignorant of military capabilities as well as the physical limitations on the use of military force. For their part, how will military leaders prepare their forces in the inevitable ambiguities that will flow from civilian leaders ignorant of the complexities involved in the use of force?

What the nation can hope from its government, civilian as well as military departments, is the ability to adapt and to provide sensible, intelligent appraisals of the kind of military actions required in what are invariably uncertain and ambiguous circumstances. Past events suggest how complex and difficult to predict those circumstances may be. Historians are still debating, even after nearly eight decades, whether Neville Chamberlain should or should not have stood up against Nazi Germany during the Czech crisis of 1938.[1] In the future, the United States and its allies cannot afford a repetition of the slapdash, incompetent planning, execution, and exit from the Iraq War of 2003–11.

Yet in looking at the larger framework through which the American military, government, and people regard the world and prepare to differentiate the existential threats from those that are merely a nuisance, there is considerable reason for worry. This is because, in the end, the most important capability lies in the degree to which one understands one's opponents, their *Weltanschauung,* their culture, their history, and their aims. Unfortunately for America's strategic and policy choices, Americans, ignorant of their own cultural and political frame of reference, have found it extraordinarily difficult to understand what Sun Tzu referred to as the other.

PREPARING INTELLECTUALLY FOR WAR

In the final analysis, the profession of arms is much more than simply fighting at the sharp end and providing needed logistics to the combat

---

1. For this author's view on the subject (that the surrender at Munich was a disaster), see Williamson Murray, *The Change in the European Balance of Power, 1938–1939, The Path to Ruin* (Princeton. NJ, 1984), particularly chs. 6, 7, and 8.

forces. It is, as previous chapters have emphasized, a matter of studying war as well as training and exercising tactical and operational
capabilities. General Mattis once commented in an e-mail shortly
before the invasion of Iraq in fall 2002 that Alexander the Great

> would not be in the least perplexed by the enemy we face right
> now in Iraq, and our leaders going into this fight do their troops
> a disservice by not studying (studying, vice just reading) the men
> who have gone before us. We have been fighting on this planet
> for 5,000 years and we should take advantage of their experi-
> ence. "Winging" it and filling body bags as we sort out what
> works reminds us of the moral dictates and the cost of incompe-
> tence in our profession.[2]

There are examples from the past, especially from the twenties
and thirties, that suggest how the US military needs to prepare its
forces over the coming decades. While the United States minimized
its expenditures on its military during the interwar period, the army
and the navy took the intellectual preparation of their officer corps
far more seriously than was the case with any other nation during
that period.[3] The United States reaped enormous dividends from
the intellectual preparation of the services' officer corps during the
war, because the military profession is not only the most demanding
physically of all the professions, it is also the most demanding intel-

---

2. Unpublished e-mail, quoted with permission from General Jim Mattis.

3. For the importance of professional military education and its influence on
the culture of the US Navy in the interwar period, see Williamson Murray, "US
Naval Strategy and Japan," in Williamson Murray and Richard Hart Sinnreich,
Successful Strategies: Triumphing in War and Peace from Antiquity to the Present (Cambridge, 2013).

lectually. During times of peace it cannot replicate much of the chaos, chance, and confusion that characterize the battlefield. As Michael Howard has pointed out:

> There arc two great difficulties with which the professional soldier, sailor, or airman has to contend with in equipping himself as commander. First his profession is almost unique in that he may have to exercise it once in a lifetime, if indeed that often. . . . Secondly the complex problem of running a [military organization] at all is liable to occupy his mind and skill so completely that it is easy to forget what it is being run for.[4]

Admiral Chester Nimitz, who commanded the joint forces in the war in the Central Pacific, commented on his return to the United States that the war gaming at the Naval War College in Newport and the fleet exercises had enabled the navy to foresee everything that it would confront in the conflict against the Japanese except for the kamikazes. Other senior leaders, Dwight Eisenhower in particular, emphasized the importance of their intellectual preparation in the period before the war. Ironically, when the war was over, in spite of the fact that senior leaders emphasized how crucial their time at the war colleges and staff colleges had been, professional military education slid into the backwaters of service concerns.[5]

---

4. Michael Howard, "The Uses and Abuses of Military History," in Michael Howard, *The Causes of War and Other Essays* (Cambridge, MA, 1983), pp. 188–97.

5. Admiral Raymond Spruance chose to take command of the Naval War College in Newport upon his return from command of the Fifth Fleet, although there were other supposedly "more prestigious" commands available. In that respect he followed in the path of Admiral William Sims, who upon his return from command of US naval forces in Europe during the First World War assumed command of the Naval War College.

There were several causes for this decline in the study of the wider aspects of the conduct of war. Throughout the Cold War, from 1947 through 1990, the US military was on a war footing, if not at war. The Korean conflict underlined that the nuclear shield had not prevented the need for substantial conventional forces to deter aggression at levels that did not demand an immediate nuclear response. But the preparation of those forces did not demand a great deal of intellectual thought, since much of the focus was on defending Europe. After all, the enemy remained the same, while the strategic framework of a bipolar world did not seem all that complex and difficult to understand.

But the most important factor was that a substantial number of officers who had entered the services in the mid- to late 1930s had been too young to attend the staff colleges, much less the war colleges. They returned at the war's end as colonels and in some cases brigadier generals. Many had the attitude that Colonel William Westmoreland expressed when asked whether he was interested in attending the Army War College as a student in the late 1940s. The colonel indicated that he was perfectly willing to serve on the faculty but saw no reason to attend as a student. After all, he had had extensive combat experience in the war. Unfortunately, he did not understand that his combat experience, as well as his education at West Point, would do little to prepare him for the political and operational challenges of war in the 1960s. In South Vietnam he conducted military operations entirely different from the conventional warfare that the American military had been emphasizing in the period after the Second World War, given the nature of the Soviet threat.

Moreover, a general weakening of an intellectual understanding of war and strategy in its widest sense had emerged among US military leaders by the early 1960s. Senior military officers displayed little ability to deal with Robert McNamara, the new secretary of defense, in matters of strategy. The result was a failure to argue intelligently against the secretary's and the president's bizarre and dishonest approach to the decision to commit US troops to the defense of South Vietnam. The failure created a needless and disastrous American intervention in a war the French had already lost in 1954 at Dien Bien Phu.[6] The lack of a coherent understanding of the conflict's strategic and political framework or the nature of the war showed in how Westmoreland conducted the war in South Vietnam. By 1972 and the removal of US ground forces from Vietnam, the war had created a deeply divided nation in the United States, while the military, especially the army and marine corps, hovered on the brink of collapse.

How the military recovered is one of the great stories in American military history. The shift to an all-volunteer army removed the worst aspects of a conscript military, while slowly but steadily the services weeded out the incompetent officers and NCOs, the drug addicts, and the criminals.[7] The process took much of the 1970s. With the increasingly disciplined forces came a wave of technologically advanced weapons, aimed at fighting a high-end conflict against the Soviet Union in Central Europe. But even more important was that the services established instrumented ranges for their training.

---

6. The wretched story is told by H. R. McMaster, *Dereliction of Duty: Lyndon Johnson, Robert McNamara, the Joint Chiefs of Staff, and the Lies That Led to Vietnam* (New York, 1997). The French had already lost the first Vietnam War against the Viet Minh from 1947 to 1954.

7. A number of marine and army officers who were junior officers in the early to mid-1970s have told me that they and their NCOs would not go into the barracks unless they were carrying loaded pistols. Such was the undisciplined and mutinous atmosphere that existed among the enlisted soldiers and marines.

TOP GUN for the navy and RED FLAG for the air force provided realistic training for pilots and aircrews. The navy's program, instituted before the Linebacker assaults on North Vietnam in 1972, significantly improved the performance of navy fighter pilots in air-to-air combat against North Vietnamese fighter pilots.[8] For the army, the National Training Center at Fort Irwin changed its approach to training and made preparing troops for combat far more realistic, as did the marine corps training center at Twentynine Palms. The impressive performance of US forces against the Iraqis in the Gulf War of 1991 underlined how effectively the new training regime had been at preparing them to handle conventional, high-intensity conflict.

Unfortunately for America's strategic choices in the first decades of the twenty-first century, the services did little to improve the performance of professional military education (pme) in the period after Vietnam. Unlike the training regime, which prepares combat forces on the sharp end to fight and on which the services placed such emphasis, pme aims to prepare the officer corps for the difficulties involved in conducting war at the operational and strategic levels. Admiral Stansfield Turner, who carried out radical reforms at the Naval War College in the early 1970s, which turned that institution into the finest academic institution for the study of strategy in the world, noted to the author his conception of what pme should aim at achieving:

---

8. During Rolling Thunder, 1965–68, the exchange ratio between navy fighters and North Vietnamese fighters was one US aircraft lost for two North Vietnamese. In 1972 during Linebacker I and II, the ratio was twelve North Vietnamese aircraft for each navy aircraft.

War colleges are places to educate the senior officer corps in the large military and strategic issues that confront America. . . . They should educate these officers by a demanding intellectual curriculum to think in wider terms than their busy operational careers have thus far demanded. Above all the war colleges should broaden the intellectual and military horizons of the officers who attend, so that they have a conception of the larger strategic and operational issues that confront our military and our nation.[9]

There were some improvements to pme in the post-Vietnam era. Turner radically transformed the curriculum of the Naval War College, but his efforts were an exception.[10] Unfortunately, the navy then and now has followed a path of rarely sending its future leaders to its own war college. In addition to Turner's changes, in the early 1980s, the army, under General Don Starry, commander of the Training and Doctrine Command, drove the creation of a second-year program at the Command and Staff College. The School of Advanced Military Studies educated officers to plan and conduct war at the operational level in a rigorous and intellectually impressive graduate-level education. Both the marine corps with its School of Advanced Warfighting and the air force with its School of Advanced Airpower Studies followed suit. The navy, not surpris-

---

9. Quoted in Williamson Murray, "Grading the War Colleges," *National Interest*, Winter 1986/1987.

10. The author has taught over three different periods at the Naval War College in the Strategy and Policy course and used its format to introduce a similar course at The Ohio State University. Professor Peter Mansoor has continued to teach that course at that institution. Professors Paul Kennedy and John Gaddis teach a similar course at Yale.

ingly, given its attitude toward pme, failed to establish a second-year program and displayed little interest in sending its officers to the second-year programs of the other services. Through to the present day, all the second-year programs have remained rigorous, graduate-level institutions devoted to the study of war.

The picture in terms of the main schools of professional education was less impressive. The situation was so bad by the 1980s that Congress stepped in, and a subcommittee of the House Armed Services Committee under Representative Ike Skelton examined all the major schools. Skelton's report represented a stinging indictment of what was supposed to be professional military education.[11] The interviews his staff conducted with the leaders of the colleges of professional military education still make astonishing reading a quarter of a century later. Some of these institutions reflected the worst aspects of 1960s educational reform: no grades, no ranking of students, and a general belief that students should do their own thing. In fact, in the early 1980s, the Army War College was spending two and a half times more hours in studying US immigration policy than it was in having its students study the strategic framework of the First and Second World Wars and the intervening interwar period. Paul Van Riper, eventually a lieutenant general in the marine corps, commented about his experience at the Army War College in the early 1980s: "There appeared to be little opportunity for the study of *war* at this *war* college."[12]

---

11. For the full hearings, see "Professional Military Education, Hearings before the Panel on Military Education of the Committee on Armed Services," House of Representatives, One Hundredth Congress (Washington, 1990).

12. Paul K. Van Riper, "The Relevance of History to the Military Profession: An American Marine's View," in Williamson Murray and Richard Hart Sinnreich,

At the time the general attitude among the generals and admirals, when they addressed the students, was that attendance at the staff and war colleges was a period when they could rest during their busy careers and get to know their families.[13] The officers attending those institutions did not receive evaluations of their performances that were passed on to their promotion boards—nor do they receive evaluations in the present system.[14] Have matters improved? Having been an advocate of serious professional military education over the past three decades, this author's view is that there has been little significant improvement. In the end this is a particularly depressing story because, while Representative Skelton headed the House Armed Services Committee, he made every effort to help the services and their educational institutions improve the quality of the study of operations and strategy. Now that Skelton is no longer alive, it is doubtful whether another representative will devote the same amount of attention and support to military education.

What then does professional military education need to emphasize? Those who have taught in a serious, graduate-level program understand that an academic year represents a short period. The Naval War College offered the best approach; its syllabus offered over the course of a year in three trimesters an intensive study: in the first, strategy; in the second, an examination of potential uses of joint forces (the use of the four services in combination) at the

---

eds., *The Past as Prologue: The Importance of History to the Military Profession* (Cambridge, 2006), p. 45.

13. This was my experience at the Air War College, 1980–81, and the Naval War College, 1991–92.

14. In the case of the army and air force officer evaluation reports; in the case of the navy and marine corps fitreps (fitness reports).

operational level; and in the third, a study of the processes through which the president and Congress develop and decide on the defense budget. It represents a useful model the other war colleges have failed to follow.

But beyond study for war and staff colleges, the services need to emphasize to a far greater extent military and strategic history. Finally, there needs to be greater emphasis on how officers perform in their academic studies in the boards that evaluate them for promotion and choose them for command positions. Such evaluations should obviously not replace how they perform in the field but rather be combined with their tactical performance to indicate their potential for higher command. Only by so doing can the system prevent individuals like Tommy Franks and Ricardo Sanchez from rising to the highest ranks.

The price for having an officer corps unfamiliar with the wider aspects of war beyond the tactics and conduct of major combat operations became apparent in Iraq shortly after the successful takedown of Saddam Hussein's odious regime. Few of the generals on the spot recognized the rapid rise of the insurgency. One of the ironies of the emerging insurgency was the fact that the three generals who conducted the conventional invasion—Major General Buford Blount, 3rd Infantry Division; Major General David Petraeus, 101st Airborne Division; and Major General James Mattis, 1st Marine Division—were all prepared intellectually and in terms of their experience for what followed the conventional war. Blount had had extensive experience with the Saudi military; Petraeus had a PhD in government from Princeton; and Mattis was an extraordinarily well-read intellectual as well as a warrior. However, all three generals and their units had returned almost immediately to the United States by early fall 2003, where their expertise played little role in staunching the insurgency at its beginning. The task of policing up an increasingly messy situation fell to new generals, few of whom appear to have prepared themselves to adapt to the war American forces actually had to fight.

Outside the new leader of Central Command, General John Abizaid, the majority of the general officers and colonels who assumed control of the occupation of Iraq possessed neither the background nor the capacity to adapt to a situation that was rapidly heading south. In an e-mail to the author, Colonel Peter Mansoor, commander of one of the 1st Armored Division's brigades during the first year of the occupation of Bagdad, noted:

Too many leaders (both civilian and military) at the highest level [brigade commander and above] or those positioned in staffs at operational headquarter or in strategic executive branch positions were excessively involved in what was happening in tactical units at the expense of developing a long-term strategy and operational concept to implement it. . . . There was little conception of the operational art at CJTF-7.[15] Units initially occupied zones that transcended local government boundaries. . . . Military units were more or less distributed evenly across Iraq, even though it soon became apparent that the heart of the insurgency lay in the Sunni Triangle. . . . Shortage of forces, lack of vision, or lack of will prevented a more permanent presence in

---

15. Combined Joint Task Force 7.

the area and an effective plan to deal with Fallujah until after it had become a symbol for the insurgency.[16]

It is essential for military organizations to understand the nature of the war upon which they have embarked as well as the political and military context within which that conflict is taking place. The experiences of Iraq offers up a sobering warning, especially because the future commitment and deployment of US military forces in coming decades remains so uncertain and ambiguous. One cannot forecast whether those forces will find themselves committed to a war in East Asia, South Asia, the Middle East, or even the Baltic. Nor can one forecast the political context or the military balance of power. Inevitably, US commanders, their staffs, and those on the sharp end are going to have to adapt to the fact that they will discover that many of their assumptions going into the war will be flawed or wrong.[17]

That is not necessarily a mark of incompetence but rather the reality that no military organization in history has ever entered a war fully prepared for the next war. Instead, the truly competent and effective militaries adapt to the reality that they confront rather than attempting to make reality fit their prewar assumptions. Moreover, since the enemy always gets a vote, effective military organizations must continue to adapt, because the enemy is adapting as well.[18] But

---

16. Colonel Peter Mansoor's e-mail to the author, quoted with his permission.

17. For a discussion of the problems associated with adaptation in war through the ages see, Williamson Murray, *Military Adaptation in War: With Fear of Change* (Cambridge, 2013).

18. Ibid.

the most important factor is an understanding of the political and strategic framework within which a conflict is occurring. In the Vietnam War, the United States may have won every battle at the tactical level, but that proved irrelevant because the North Vietnamese won at the political and strategic levels. Moreover, Ho Chi Minh also won the battle of the narrative not only in South Vietnam, but, more important, in the United States itself as well as among America's allies in Europe.

Again, one must ask whether matters have changed. The great Anglo-American strategist Colin Gray suggests they have not. The following is his devastating critique of the American military over the past decade and a half since 9/11.

> With their much-trumpeted transformation geared to enable them to scale ever higher heights of military excellence in battle, the US Armed Forces have committed three cardinal sins against the eternal lore of war. First, they have confused military with strategic success. The former is about defeating the forces of the foe: the latter is about using that defeat to advance the goals of policy. Second, the US Armed Forces have confused combat with war. When the regular style of fighting concludes, the war may, or may not, be over. Also, there is far more to war than combat. Just how strategically decisive military success will prove to be will depend on how holistic an understanding of war has been adopted. Third, as an extension of the second point, the US Armed Forces are especially prone to neglect the timeless maxim that war is about peace, not about itself.[19]

---

19. Gray, *Another Bloody Century*, p. 189.

One hopes that the future will prove him wrong. In fairness to the military, however, policy makers in Washington have often proved deeply flawed in their political and strategic directions to the military. After all, the Iraq insurgency arose out of injudicious, ill-thought-out policies such as de-Ba'athification and the complete disarming of the Iraqi military, directed from the highest level of the American government. Nevertheless, there were few objections from senior military leaders. In retrospect America's military leadership must be prepared intellectually to adapt to the political and strategic context in the next war, or it will inevitably face a drawn-out war of attrition which the United States cannot afford.

THE GROWING SCLEROSIS OF BUREAUCRACY

Perhaps the most dangerous trend in the US military at present is the increasing size of the bureaucratic organizations that are responsible for organizing and running the vast establishments for which the joint commands and the services are responsible, whether military or civilian. Bureaucracies are, of course, essential for the functioning of any modern society. The business of running any major military organization in peacetime with its enormous complexity, not to mention the problem of deploying large numbers of troops and military equipment over great distances, requires the skillful handling of staffs and organizational skill. Yet bureaucracies also represent a considerable problem in the developing of imaginative approaches to innovation and the skillful employment of military forces.

As the historian MacGregor Knox has noted:

Bureaucracies are neatly *zweckrational*: swift and precise—in theory and often in practice—in executing orders. But they inevitably define national purpose in terms of bureaucratic rather than national survival. They are happiest with established wisdom and incremental change. They cherish the myth that virtually all strategic problems are soluble in and through their own element—be it diplomacy, economic power, covert knowledge and action, ground combat, naval supremacy, or air bombardment—and that problems not thus soluble are not problems. When faced with the incommensurate or unquantifiable alternatives that are the stuff of strategy, they usually retreat to incoherent compromise with their fellows or take flight into strategy by intuition—unless the structure of decision making forces them to defend all choices in rational terms. And in the absence of driving political leadership, even structured debate may produce only paralysis.[20]

The case study of the potential of the Spitfire to serve as a long-range escort fighter suggests how destructive military cultures and their bureaucracies can prove. In 1941 Winston Churchill asked Sir Charles Portal, the chief of air staff, whether it might be possible to design and build a long-range escort fighter so that Bomber Command could carry out its offensive against Germany during the day and thereby achieve far greater accuracy. The air marshal replied

---

20. Williamson Murray, MacGregor Knox, and Alvin Bernstein, *The Making of Strategy: Rulers, States, and War* (Cambridge, 1992), pp. 615–16.

that such an aircraft was technologically infeasible. Churchill quite rightly replied that that state of affairs "closed many doors."[21]

In fact, Portal was wrong. Such a fighter already existed, namely, the reconnaissance Spitfire, which, carrying approximately the same weight as the fighter version with its cameras taking the place of the fighter's machine guns, was flying all the way to Berlin. Because the culture of the bureaucracy of the Royal Air Force (RAF) staff believed that long-range escort fighters were impossible to build, its members persisted in refusing to examine the possibility. Even when American engineers in 1944 at Wright Paterson Field turned two Spitfires into long-range escort fighters that managed to fly back across the Atlantic, the RAF's leadership rejected a reality that contradicted its fundamental assumption that a long-range fighter was an impossibility. Air Vice Marshal John Breakey, assistant chief of the air staff technical requirements, actually claimed in a letter passed to Portal that the Americans had "removed one of the main former ribs from the wing roots, and this has reduced the strength of the wing to a degree which lowers the factors below acceptable limitations for combat."[22] In fact the Americans had done no such thing in their adding additional fuel tanks to the Spitfire. Breakey was either entirely ignorant of the situation, rather unlikely given his position, or in British terms being economical with the truth (in American terms, flat-out lying).

---

21. Sir Charles Webster and Noble Frankland, *The Strategic Air Offensive against Germany*, vol. 1, *Preparation* (London, 1980), p. 177.

22. The astonishing story is told seven decades after its occurrence (a sad comment on the competence of historians) in David Stubbs, "A Blind Spot? The Royal Air Force (RAF) and Long-Range Fighters, 1936–1944," *Journal of Military History*, April 2014.

For the most part such bureaucratic assumptions did not hinder the conduct of the war by the British throughout the Second World War. There are, however, worrisome trends in the American government. The massive expansion of the National Security Council's (NSC's) bureaucracy has created an organization incapable of providing reasonable advice to the president. The numbers involved in that council are staggering. Membership in the NSC, besides the president, includes six statutory members, four regular attendees (the national security adviser, the White House chief of staff, the deputy national security adviser, and the attorney general), and seven additional participants such as the secretary of the treasury. The NSC's director with the title of assistant to the president for national security affairs (Susan Rice) has under her four deputy assistants, who in turn have no less than twenty-two special assistants to the president, all with innumerable worker bees, few, if any, of whom speak a foreign language or know much about the history and background of the areas they are charged with following.[23]

The management philosophy that created the NSC is typical of the whole system of American government. It appears to rest on the belief that a grouping of ninety staff officers or civilian analysts because of their combined IQs will be able to produce "work" on the level of an Einstein or a George Kennan. In fact what such bureaucracies produce is watered-down mush that represents the collected average with, of course, a number of pet rocks thrown in

---

23. A friend, who is an expert on Russian and German history, was recently asked to give a background talk to a number of analysts at the NSC on the historical framework of current problems in Eastern and Central Europe. He characterized the questions he got from his audience for the most part as revealing a fundamental ignorance of the area.

for good measure. As Knox points out at the beginning of this section, such bureaucratic organizations are incapable of providing imaginative, out-of-the-box assessments that challenge basic assumptions because by their very nature they aim at consensus rather than confrontation and argument.

The bureaucratization of the military owes its origins to other difficulties than that of the NSC. Perhaps the greatest hurdle that confronts the services in attempting to adapt to the problems raised by war in the twenty-first century lies in personnel systems that rest on laws and concepts established at the end of the Second World War. For all intents and purposes, that framework reflects the antiquated, lockstep approach to personnel management of General Motors of the early 1950s. In other words, those who stay in the narrow track of their career fields and do little or nothing to prepare themselves for the wider responsibilities of thinking about joint operations or strategy are those whom the service personnel systems reward. In the army a few, like Petraeus and H. R. McMaster, presently on active duty as a lieutenant general, slip through to high command, but they are the exception.[24]

If the services suffer from creeping bureaucratization, their problems in this regard are nothing close to those of the bureaucratic

---

24. One of the other aspects of the personnel systems is that the health profiles on the early 1950s helped drive their philosophy. The culture of the time in which officers drank and smoked heavily was such that the services had every reason to push their officers to retire at the twenty-year point (or twenty-three-year point for colonels) because of bad health. Given today's improvement in conditioning, the removal of smoking as a major factor, and the emphasis on healthy lifestyles, most officers retiring at the age of forty-five are as healthy as those who were thirty years old in 1950. Thus, the present personnel system and its financial inducements are encouraging a substantial number of officers to retire whose level of competence and knowledge is in some cases irreplaceable.

culture that America's intelligence agencies have created. In effect, they are supposed to provide the essential intelligence on which policy makers will evaluate the nature of the threats that the United States confronts. One would suppose that its analysts would understand the culture, language, politics, and history of the nations or areas for which they are responsible. Yet as recently as May 2009 *only 13 percent* of the CIA's analysts spoke or read a second language beyond English.[25] One expert on the Italian political situation asked the members of the CIA's desk on Italy how they could do their job when none of them spoke Italian. He received the reply that they could get what they needed translated. He then discovered that none of the team knew that each major Italian political party had its own newspapers, which laid out the current party's estimates on the political situation.

The differing estimates on the size of the Soviet economy and defense expenditures between the CIA and Andrew Marshall's Office of Net Assessment in the 1970s and 1980s present an interesting perspective on the difference between bureaucratic intelligence and intelligence developed by a small number of individuals working outside the system. The Office of Net Assessment has been in existence since 1972 and consists of fewer than twenty serving officers and civilians at any given time.[26] Throughout the Cold War, the number of CIA analysts working on the Soviet

---

25. Of those who were deployed outside the United States on assignment and knew a foreign language, the percentage was 30. My sense is that the figures for state department employees are only marginally better.

26. The caliber of those who have worked as military and civilian analysts in the Office of Net Assessment is indeed extraordinary. They include Andrew Krepinevich, Barry Watts, Eliot Cohen, Steve Rosen, Aaron Friedberg, James Roche, as well as a number of consultants, who number some of America's most outstanding minds.

Union, its military, and its economy numbered in the hundreds, if not thousands. In the mid-1970s the CIA was estimating that the Soviets were spending between only 6 and 7 percent of their gross national product (GNP) on their military. Marshall and his analysts, however, came up with a much higher estimate of between 10 and 20 percent. The argument between the CIA and Net Assessment continued into the 1980s, when the collapse of the Soviet Union underlined how inaccurate the CIA's estimates were and how close to reality Net Assessment's calculations had been.

Exacerbating the CIA's underestimates was the fact that the agency miscalculated the size of the Soviet economy: instead of being 50 to 60 percent of US GNP, it was in fact barely 25 percent the size of the American economy. This meant that the Soviets were spending 30 to 40 percent of GNP on their military forces—a major factor in the Soviet Union's collapse. What explains the fact that the Office of Net Assessment got it right and the CIA got it wrong is the fact that Marshall's office was able to reach out to experts outside the government's bureaucracy and had the freedom to deal with uncomfortable realities without the pressure of the groupthink that characterizes most bureaucracies.

Adding to the problem of basic ignorance of foreign language and culture in the intelligence agencies are the security requirements drawn up by unimaginative, dull bureaucrats. At present they prevent individuals who may have relatives living in countries or areas, controlled by those hostile to the United States, from obtaining security clearances and thus from applying their cultural and linguistic capabilities to help the United States understand what is actually transpiring in areas where a real sense of the culture and knowledge of local politics is essential. How the United States is going to evaluate the complex and contradictory political situations with such fundamental ignorance underlying its intelligence efforts is beyond the scope of this author.[27]

Moreover, American governments have displayed a consistent inability to appoint first-class talent—which is often available—to important positions where some knowledge and competence would seem to be a basic requirement. The most obvious cases of individuals holding positions for which they have no discernable qualifications have involved political appointees. In the early days of the occupation of Iraq, large numbers of young people with connections to the Republican National Committee received appointments for which they had no qualifications. The Obama administration has followed the same path. The *Wall Street Journal* headline for its story on the state department's spokeswomen, Jennifer Psaki and Marie Harf, was "Lucy and Ethel Take Foggy Bottom." But appointments within the bureaucracy are often more damaging. One might particularly note the appointment of Christopher Hill to be ambassador to Baghdad in 2009. Hill was a state department bureaucrat who did not speak Arabic and completely misunderstood the political situation in Iraq. The cascade of events that followed directly resulted in the arrival of ISIS throughout much of northern Iraq.[28]

---

27. The current situation is worth contrasting with the experience of the British and US intelligence agencies which reached out and recruited extraordinarily competent individuals to serve in their ranks. The extent to which they went and the rewards they reaped is suggested by the fact that a twenty-one-year-old Cambridge undergraduate history major, Harry Hinsley, joined Bletchley Park in September 1939, and within a year and a half would be one of the most important analysts of the Kriegsmarine and play a crucial role in the breaking into of the German naval codes with a major impact in the Battle of the Atlantic.

28. For the sorry story, see Emma Sky, *The Unraveling: High Hopes and Missed Opportunities in Iraq* (New York, 2015).

We might leave our discussion of the pernicious impact of what I have taken to calling the security Nazis. For those who live normal lives outside the range of the federal government's bureaucracy, the best example of such bureaucratic incompetence is the transportation security administration.[29] But the bureaucratic consequence of the security Nazis is that the defense department's security system more often than not lacks any common sense. After the deluge of classified materials released by Edward Snowden appeared on the Internet, the department's bureaucrats forbade anyone using a government computer to access the Snowden material to see what he had leaked because the material was still classified. How then, one might have asked, were department employees supposed to deal with the leakages? Well that was obviously someone else's problem to solve.

RULES OF ENGAGEMENT

The bureaucratization of America's military has combined with a tightening of the legal restraints that govern the use of military force. It is perhaps in the nature of the small wars and terrorism in which we have found ourselves engaged over the past several decades that rules of engagement have increasingly limited the use of military force. Undoubtedly the almost ubiquitous presence of

---

29. An example of the agency's bureaucracy occurred eight years ago when my seventy-eight-year-old mother-in-law, a little lady weighing less than 100 pounds, arrived at Dulles Airport. Because her thumbprint had been worn off due to work, TSA security individuals held her for more than five hours without informing us or allowing the airlines to indicate that she had arrived.

the media has had its influence. Nor should we discount the impact of the belief on the part of substantial portions of the US population that precision-guided weapons can largely remove the problem of killing civilians, whether innocent or not, from the equation of war.

Capabilities like Global Hawk and Predator have seemingly taken the human cost out of war, at least from our equation. Yet Americans should not forget Clausewitz's grim warning to those who believe that war can be done painlessly:

> Kind-hearted people might of course think there was some inge-
> nious way to disarm or defeat an enemy without too much blood-
> shed, and might imagine this is the true goal of the art of war.
> Pleasant as it sounds, it is a fallacy that must be exposed: war is
> such a dangerous business that the mistakes that come from kind-
> ness are the very worst.[30]

There will be blowback from our use of unmanned aerial vehicles. In some respects such blowback has already occurred in Paris, San Bernardino, and Brussels. Unseen and unheard, these drones can take out terrorists and their leaders, but they cannot remove the threat. Only the presence of ground forces can do that, and neither the current American administration nor the Europeans seem will-ing to return to that path.[31]

A young marine captain best summed up the result of the belief that the West can fight a war where no civilian casualties occur. He

---

30. Clausewitz, *On War,* p. 75.

31. In fairness to the French, it is worth noting that in December they launched their military forces into Mali against Islamic militants who had seized much of the northern part of the country.

noted that when he went out on patrol with his marines in Afghanistan, he at times felt that he was going to confront situations where if he ordered them to fire in what he judged to be a dangerous situation he had a good chance of ruining his military career before it had barely started. On the other hand if he ordered them not to fire, he was putting their lives at risk. The lawyers, politicians, and bureaucrats in the NSC so eager to ensure that the actions of the American military conform to some incalculable set of moral and humane standards do not face such hard choices.[32]

THE PROBLEM? PERHAPS IT'S
THE STATE OF AMERICA

For the most part, the American people, especially the upper-middle and upper classes, have been largely removed from any experience, even among relatives and friends, with the American military, much less the horror of war. Typical of that divide was my experience with a young senior at one of America's most prestigious colleges. Graduating *summa cum laude*, he is about to march off into one of the major law schools in the United States, with tuition running somewhere in the neighborhood of $70,000 per year, much of which he will have to finance through loans. He will then have to pay off that burden by slaving away at some major law firm like

---

32. The recent movie *Eye in the Sky,* while somewhat exaggerated in its portrayal of the technological abilities available to the US and Allied military forces, does catch the bureaucratic ability of politicians and lawyers in government service to obfuscate realistic choices and avoid hard decisions, capturing the difficulties involved in decision making by a considerable number of individuals.

Jarndyce and Jarndyce, while working out the intricacies of merg-
ers. I suggested to him that if he were to enlist in the navy's officer
candidate program and serve four years, not only would he see
something of the world, but when he left the service he could look
forward to having his entire law school tuition paid for by the US
government as well as his books and a stipend to cover most of his
living expenses. My young friend was not interested; after all, the
American military is a far-off land to be cheered and admired from
afar. In terms of those who are the main recruiting pool for the
enlisted ranks, one might note that over the past fifteen years, military pay has increased by approximately 60 percent in real terms,
so that in effect there is little or no gap with civilian pay, especially
when one considers the extraordinary retirement, health, and educational benefits.

To a considerable extent, the armed services and the coast guard
have found themselves competing for an increasingly small percentage of the cohort that graduates each year from high school.[33] The
main areas of recruitment have increasingly become small towns,
farming communities, and the children of those who are already
serving or who have served. A recent article in *Army Magazine* put
the situation in the following terms: "A societal rift is silently
and rapidly widening between America and its Army. On one side
is the Army, with a clear vision of its future that requires highly
qualified volunteers. On the other side is a youth population whose

---

33. There are, one might note, considerable differences among the services
in terms of their difficulties in filling recruiting quotas. The marine corps has had
the best success, probably because the officers and NCOs whom they select for
recruiting duty are among their most outstanding.

qualification and desire for service are quickly eroding. In the middle is a society that publicly applauds its soldiers but is not connected with, able to fund, or willing to provide real support to its army."[34]

Not surprisingly, given the inexcusable largesse the federal government is throwing at America's colleges and universities— the most incompetently run institutions in the national life—in terms of government loans, recruiters are finding it increasingly difficult to attract young, qualified males and females, whose parents and families know nothing about the military.[35] In addition, some school districts, driven by administrators and teachers unfriendly to the military, have been making it difficult for recruiters to approach students to inform them of the advantages they might gain by joining. One should also not discount the fact that the increasingly hostile media are doing little to encourage the young to enlist.[36]

Finally, one might note that Congress, for its part, is not doing much to help in the process of allowing the department of defense to spread its net more widely. In addition to the regular pool of potential recruits, there exists a pool of 700,000 young people who

---

34. Major General Allen Batschelet and Colonel Mike Runey, "The Army We Need; The Army We Can Have," *Army Magazine,* February 2014.

35. The one service where this is not true is the marine corps.

36. As Robert Kaplan has pointed out, Sergeant First Class Paul Ray Smith being nominated for and receiving the Congressional Medal of Honor for heroism was mentioned only ninety times in the media. On the other hand, the supposed abuse of the Quran at Guantanamo Bay was mentioned in the media 4,677 times, while the court-martial of Lynndie England for incidents at Abu Ghraib received 5,159 mentions in the media. Robert Kaplan, *Hog Pilots, Blue Water Grunts* (New York, 2007), p. 252.

are not eligible to enlist unless the laws prohibiting noncitizens from joining are changed.[37] Many are the children of undocumented immigrants, who are eager to serve as a means to earn their citizenship. A number of congressional representatives, who oppose allowing the services to recruit from this pool, argue that serving in the military offers too easy a path to citizenship. Not surprisingly, few of them have ever served in the military. The department of defense has received limited authority to recruit a small number of this pool, but bureaucratic obfuscation and worries about the political ramification of recruiting the children of undocumented immigrants has limited the ability to draw on this group.

There is another program—Military Accessions Vital to National Interest (MAVNI)—which aims to allow documented noncitizens with language and cultural skills to join the services. Again bureaucratic and political opposition within and outside the military has minimized the program in a tangle of red tape. Ironically, the statistics indicate that the MAVNI recruits complete their enlistments at a higher rate than other groups, have higher academic scores on average, and possess high school diplomas. One is struck by the inability of many in the US government to recognize the importance of widening the pool of potential recruits as much as possible, especially given the societal pressures that are driving too many young people to discount serving their country as a serious option. The possibility exists that, in the near future, the military will no

---

37. This is a bizarre legal impediment to enlistment, because there is a long tradition stretching back to the American Revolution of encouraging the enlistment of foreign nationals in the American military. After all, Baron von Steuben and Comte de Lafayette both played important roles in the training of American soldiers to fight the British during the Revolution.

longer be able to recruit the high-level eighteen- to twenty-one-year-olds who have given the United States such extraordinary capabilities on the battlefield.

The absence of military experience in the top levels of the US government, executive as well as congressional, has serious implications. Admittedly, the two greatest war presidents in American history, Abraham Lincoln and Franklin Roosevelt, did not serve in the military.[38] Time spent in military service is not, in the end, a prerequisite to understand the complexities of either strategy or the necessary components that go into the making of effective military institutions. After all, as Frederick the Great commented to his senior officers, who were declaiming on the importance of service in the field, the mule on the other side of the tent had spent more time on campaign than any of them, but it surely had learned nothing. Nevertheless, some familiarity with military institutions and the extraordinary difficulties under which they operate is important in dealing with the complex issues of whether or not to use military force, which will inevitably confront policy makers in the coming decades.

The last president of the United States underlines the divide that separates the American elite from the realities of much of the world. In almost every respect Barack Obama fits the *Weltanschauung* of the American upper-middle and upper classes. In terms of IQ, Obama may well be the smartest president ever to sit in the White House. But that does not make him a particularly well-

---

38. Although in fairness, one must note that Abraham Lincoln served for ninety days with the Illinois militia, where, according to him, he fought mostly mosquitoes, while Franklin Roosevelt served for eight years as the assistant secretary of the navy under Woodrow Wilson.

educated person. He appears rather to reflect the worst aspects of the collapse of American education: not interested in history or classical literature, a brilliant lawyer, speaks no foreign language, views the world as if it should conform to his standards, and believes that "ISIS is not an existential threat to the United States," while "climate change is." Apparently he has taken to commenting to his aides that "if only everyone could be like the Scandinavians, this would all be easy."[39]

Nothing better suggests the president's ignorance of history than the extensive interview he provided Jeffrey Goldberg in the April 2016 *Atlantic*. In discussing the Libyan fiasco, he noted: "We got a UN mandate, we built a coalition, it cost us $1 billion—which, when it comes to military operations, is very cheap. We averted large-scale civilian casualties, we prevented what almost surely would have been a prolonged and bloody civil conflict." Then he added, "And despite all that, Libya is a mess."[40] In his decision making, Obama seems to have entirely dismissed the second- and third-order effects, such as the appearance of long-term violence among the various tribal groups and ISIS and al Qaeda franchises in Libya, which might follow once the effort to remove Moammar Gadhafi had succeeded. "The degree of tribal division in Libya was greater than our analysts had expected. And our ability to have any kind of structure there that we could interact with and start training and start providing resources broke down very quickly."[41] In effect, the Europeans, with the full support of the United States, overthrew an

---

39. Quoted in Jeffrey Goldberg, "The Obama Doctrine," *Atlantic*, April 2016, pp. 77, 80.

40. Ibid., p. 81.

41. Ibid., p. 81

admittedly odious regime with no plan to establish stability on the ground and no willingness to intervene with ground forces, the only means to establish some form of order.

The overthrow of Gadhafi was Iraq all over again, except that the second Bush administration, having overthrown an equally nasty regime, attempted to put some of the pieces back together. Perhaps the most astonishing comment Obama made was that we no longer had to worry about the Middle East, since "thanks to America's energy revolution, [it] will soon be of negligible relevance to the U.S. economy." Again this represents the worst kind of linear thinking, because a collapse of the Middle East would ultimately lead to a collapse of the global economy and drive US energy prices through the roof. At a minimum, a collapse in the Middle East would make America's energy revolution irrelevant. Moreover, it is not exactly as if the president has done much to help the supposed US energy revolution with his sabotaging of the Keystone pipeline. The fecklessness of both the Americans and the Europeans toward the problems of the Middle East, not to mention Afghanistan, has gone a long way toward making war and violence much more likely throughout the world in the coming decades.

There is a larger point here. Over the past two decades, American leaders have failed in their attempts to achieve their strategic goals. In the end, those goals do not appear to have been realistic, largely because of their ignorance of the culture and politics of the region into which they committed American forces. But the military leaders seem not for the most part to have questioned those goals, nor did they articulate alternatives. But then, like their political masters, too many of them lacked the understanding of past conflicts to enable them to question the assumptions about the future use of military force.

Whatever Obama's intellectual weaknesses, they reflect the fruits of the disaster that has been America's educational system over the past half century. The history departments of America's universities and colleges have become gated communities for individuals who have spent their entire lives in the schoolhouse as students and then as professors. Serious history—and by that I mean political, diplomatic, military, and social history—has been reduced in the American academic world to the study of social, gender, or racial history. No matter how valuable such insights might be, they do nothing to prepare the future leaders of the United States to understand the world they face. Thus, the dark markers of human history, which Thucydides so brilliantly illuminated, do not occur to those who have no interest in the past that matters in thinking about strategy and the cultures that lie beyond the Western world. The world to them is new, with few guideposts or warnings. So, any road to the future will do. Such understanding has the extraordinary danger of entirely misunderstanding or misinterpreting the actions of adversarial powers.

Equally distressing has been the collapse of the study of great literature among the English and literature departments in American universities and colleges, because either such books were written by dead white males or because there are no longer any standards to judge great literature by, and therefore everything is of equal value. In a speech to the leaders of CENTCOM in 1997, Robert Kaplan underlined that the present approach to the study of great literature in higher education, not to mention our high schools, was removing one of the key components through which future generations could view and understand the unfolding world. By focusing intensely on textual details rather than the clash of personalities or the beauty of language, literature professors have turned their discipline into a baffling puzzle bereft of interest for most students. After all, anyone who has read and grasped Euripides's *Medea* can understand the madness that can grasp human beings at various times.

Even more to the point, Aeschylus's brilliant trilogy, the *Oresteia,* lays out the inherent and fierce tension in a Greek world transitioning from clan and tribe with their blood feuds and their fundamental commitment and loyalty to the family, to the state, which assumes responsibility for protecting those who are its members. So, too, Sophocles's dark tragedy *Antigone* draws out the conflict between the individual and the state. Mario Cuomo noted during the Bush-Dukakis presidential debates of 1988 that if his wife were murdered and raped, he would want to take out a baseball bat and beat the perpetrator to death, but that is why states have laws and police, precisely to prevent individuals from taking the law into their own hands. In the modern world, justice is a matter for the appointed officials, not for the individual. As Charles Hill points out, "the line between primeval and civil society is clear from all these points in the *Oresteia* and all are visibly contested today in parts of the world where civil society has not taken hold or has slipped backward."[42] Those who have no interest or education in the classics are ill-prepared to understand the fact that across the Middle East, for example, because the politics of clans, tribes, and families drive

---

42. Charles Hill, *Grand Strategies: Literature, Statecraft, and World Order* (Yale, 2010), p. 16.

human interactions in the area in the same sense that they drove societies before modern states assumed responsibility for the well-being and discipline of the citizenry.[43]

As for Aeschylus, he permanently marked himself as a true dead white male by what is written on his stele. There is no mention of his great contribution to literature with his tragedies, only this: "Beneath this stone lies Aeschylus . . . of his noble prowess the grove of Marathon can speak, and the long-haired Persian knows it well." In other words, Aeschylus counted himself a warrior first and above all. Of course, to the modern literati he was a soldier defending a city-state in which women had no vote and the slave population was close in numbers to those who were free. Thus, Aeschylus is of no more note than those who write poetry on subway cars. Ironically, given American policies in the Middle East, Aeschylus and Sophocles have more to say about the embedded conflicts in that area than the world of academic area studies. If one has never read the Greek tragedies and come to grips with their implications, then one has lost one of the great tools for understanding the fundamental human conundrum that lies between loyalty to clan or to the state. The clear warning is that if one removes the state, no matter how imperfect, without ensuring that it is replaced, one will get what the Americans and the Europeans got in Libya, but those who will truly suffer from the sloppiness of Western policies are the Libyan people.

---

43. For a three-year period, I taught a graduate seminar at George Washington. The students were for the most part drawn from some of America's greatest universities, and each year I asked them how many had read or studied a Greek tragedy in their classes. Each year the result was a depressingly few—perhaps on the order of less than 10 percent.

THE UNANSWERABLE QUESTIONS

Yet for all the difficulties that American armed forces confront now and in the near future, their training remains by far and away the most effective of all the world's military organizations. The question emerging at present is whether the United States can afford the immense expense entailed in the projection of military power to far off countries about which Americans know little.[44] Moreover, the growing divide between the general population and elites on one side and those who bear the psychological and physical burdens of defending the country on the other creates a dangerous situation. Madeleine Albright's infamous remark to General Colin Powell is worth recalling: "What's the point of you [sic] saving this superb military for, if we can't use it?"[45] The United States has received the warning from its strategic and political mistakes in Iraq and Libya with the careless use of military force, but whether its future leaders will remember that warning ten years from now is open to some doubt, given the track record of its past leaders.

A financial collapse would make it extraordinarily difficult to continue the budgetary support for the department of defense at the present rate. On the other hand, as entitlements and debt servicing steadily eat into the disposable income of the federal government, will Americans cut back on the financial support they expect from the government to fund a defense budget that provides the

---

44. In a speech during the Czech crisis of 1938, Neville Chamberlain, prime minister of Britain, commented: "How horrible, fantastic, incredible it is, that we should be digging trenches . . . because of a quarrel in a faraway country between people of whom we know nothing."

45. Madeleine Albright, *Madam Secretary: A Memoir* (New York, 2003), p. 182.

reasonable capabilities that a dangerous world requires? There are also the considerable retirement obligations that the United States owes those who have served in the military, and they are steadily growing.

We close this chapter with two nightmare scenarios from the past that may seem far-fetched, but are possibilities, given the fact that history, if it does not repeat itself, still has the annoying habit of rhyming.[46] The first is historical, the second literary, but they suggest the possibilities that might appear, if the divide between the elites and those who serve continues on its current path.

In the middle of the fourth century BC, the Athenians, who had largely restored their strategic position after their disastrous defeat in the Peloponnesian War (431–404 BC), found themselves in a desperate military situation. Caught by a more numerous Macedonian navy near the island of Amorgos in the southeastern Aegean, the Athenian admirals surrendered their fleet after only a brief skirmish in which they lost a few ships. In the history of the previous 150 years, nothing like this had ever occurred. At several occasions during their long rule, the Athenians had gone down fighting to the end: in Egypt against the Persians in the mid-fifth century BC; in Sicily at Syracuse in 413 BC; and at Aegospotami in 405 BC.

The Macedonians escorted the Athenians back to Athens, where the two sides made peace. One might say more accurately that the Athenian elite surrendered the independence of their polis to the Macedonians. The terms ended Athens' period as a great power. The upper classes, tired of the burdens of remaining a great power

---

46. Mark Twain supposedly quipped (in fact he did not) that "history does not repeat itself, but it rhymes."

in the Aegean and eastern Mediterranean, succumbed without any effort to defend the state. Moreover, they persuaded the Macedonians to exile the entire body of the thetes: the lower classes and vocal supporters of the democracy, on whom the burden of rowing the triremes fell. From this point, there would remain no rowers to drive the triremes. The historian John Hale records the results:

> Land was to be provided for the exiles in Thrace, that harsh northern country that so many Athenians of previous generations had died trying to win. Helpless the citizens packed up their households and made their way down to Piraeus for the embarkation. All around hundreds of triremes and other warships rested in their shipsheds, but their time was over. Without the harmony that had drawn the Athenians together for a common purpose, the ships were so many lifeless hulks of timber and pitch. . . . When they surrendered to the Macedonians, the Athenians had more ships and a better-equipped naval base than ever before. Philo's arsenal was still brand-new. Some mysterious essence, however, had vanished.[47]

Our secondary tale comes from the preface of Jean Lartéguy's novel about the Algerian War. The preface, however, purports to be a letter from a centurion, who has spent his life defending the frontiers of the Roman Empire but who has heard that those back in Rome no longer have any interest in the efforts and sacrifices of those who have been defending them.

---

47. John R. Hale, *Lords of the Sea: The Epic Story of the Athenian Navy and the Birth of Democracy* (New York, 2009), pp. 317–18.

We have been told, on leaving our native soil, that we were going to defend the sacred rights conferred on us by so many of our citizens settled overseas, so many years of our presence, so many benefits brought by us to populations in need of our assistance and our civilization.

We were able to verify that this was true, and, because it was true, we did not hesitate to shed our quota of blood, to sacrifice our youth and our hopes. We regretted nothing, but whereas we over here are inspired by this frame of mind, I am told that in Rome factions and conspiracies are rife, the treachery flourishes, and that many people in their uncertainty and confusion lend a ready ear to the dire temptations of relinquishment and vilify our actions.

I cannot believe all this is true and yet recent wars have shown how pernicious such a state of mind could be and to where it could lead.

Make haste to reassure me, I beg you, and tell me that our fellow citizens understand us, support us and protect us as we ourselves are protecting the glory of the empire.

If it should be otherwise, we should have to leave our bleached bones in the desert sands in vain, then beware of the anger of the Legions!

Marcus Flavinus
Centurion in the Second Cohort of the Augusta Legion
To his cousin Tertullus in Rome.[48]

---

48. Jean Lartéguy, *The Centurions* (New York, 1961), preface.

6

WHEN THE LIGHTS GO OFF

The United States and War in the
Twenty-First Century

Spartans, in the course of my life I have taken part in many wars, and I see among you people of the same age as I am. They and I have had experience, and so we are not likely to share in what may be a general enthusiasm for war, nor to think that war is a good thing or a safe thing.

Thucydides, *On War*

IN MID-JUNE 1944 THE US NAVY LAUNCHED THE AMPHIBIOUS landing forces of the US marine corps and army against the Japanese-held Mariana Islands. Admiral Raymond Spruance's Fifth Fleet represented the greatest accumulation of naval power the world had ever seen to that point. To understand the extent of that effort beyond a mere cataloguing of seven heavy carriers, eight light carriers, seven battleships, and twenty heavy and light cruisers, not to mention the innumerable support vessels and landing craft, one might look to what it took to support that fleet. Forty-six tankers accompanied the naval, ground, and air forces deployed in the operation. Those tankers dispersed "4,496,156 barrels of standard oil, 8,000,000 gallons of aviation fuel, and 275,000 barrels of diesel (overall supply being equal to 715,000 metric tons)." In effect the fuel that the Fifth Fleet used in its operations of approximately two weeks in support of the amphibious operations around the Mariana Islands and the fleet Battle of the Philippine Sea against the Imperial Japanese Navy equaled approximately three-quarters of the highest monthly total of fuel produced by the German war economy that same year in 1944.[1]

Since the Civil War, the American way of war has been about the projection of US military power over great distances.[2] In the war to preserve the United States, Union operations projected military power over the continental distances of the Confederacy, an area that encompassed some 780,000 square miles, a greater expanse than the territories of Spain, France, Britain, the Low Countries, Italy, and Germany combined. In comparison, Britain today occupies only 80,823 square miles.

But the most significant aspect of America's strategic geography has lain in the fact that two great oceans have separated it from whatever troubles might arise in Asia and particularly in Europe. In the early days of the Republic that represented crucial strategic protection, but in the twentieth century that distance provided both disadvantages as well as advantages. North America remained far removed from the world's trouble spots. But if the United States were to participate in the global power politics that exploded on the

---

1. Phillips Payson O'Brien. *How the War Was Won: Air-Sea Power and Allied Victory in World War II* (Cambridge, 2015), p. 421.

2. For a discussion of continental distances and their effect on the American Civil War, see Williamson Murray and Wayne Hsieh, *A Savage War: A Military History of the Civil War* (Princeton, NJ, 2016).

international scene at the beginning of the twentieth century with the combination of the Industrial Revolution and the French Revolution, it was going to have to project its military and economic power across oceanic distances.

In the First World War the United States had only to move its military forces across the Atlantic to the safe havens provided by its French and British allies, an effort that the Germans believed would take three years. It took only sixteen months before US troops began arriving in French ports. In the Second World War matters were not as easy. In the Pacific, with its immense distances, victory required the buildup of a logistical structure on a scale never before seen. The task in Europe was equally daunting, because it required massive support for US forces engaged in the Mediterranean and European Theaters of Operation on the ground, commitment of the Eighth and Fifteenth Air Forces to the strategic bombing of Germany, support for the Royal Navy and Royal Canadian Navy in the Battle of the Atlantic, as well as vast military and resource aid to support America's allies in the war against the Germans. But in the end, the projection of American power across the great distances of the Pacific and Atlantic Oceans, based on undreamed of logistical capabilities, allowed the United States and the Allies to crush the Axis powers.

Significantly, for virtually the whole of the Cold War, US forces remained forward-deployed. Since 1991, however, the slow but steady removal of ground and air units from Europe has created a situation analogous to that of 1941, when, with the exception of undermanned units scattered across Pacific islands, the military forces of the United States found themselves deployed within the continental United States. Thus, strategists and planners in the American military in the twenty-first century once again confront the problem of projecting military power over the vast distances of the Pacific and Atlantic Oceans. This is not new, and the services are increasingly becoming familiar with sudden deployments of their forces over great distances.

But what will be new will be the lack of forward-deployed logistical support and base structures throughout much of the world—particularly in Europe and the Middle East—with which the American military has been familiar during and after the Cold War. The base structures have been particularly important even with the withdrawal of troops, because their logistical support has proven crucial for the movement and support of US forces to the Middle East over the past decade.[3] That will not be so much the case in Asia, considering China's efforts to turn everyone in Asia into an American ally as well as the access to America's island bases that stretch across the Pacific. Nevertheless, any conflict in Asia that involves Chinese military forces will take place on China's home field, and America's military forces will find themselves dependent on logistical support stretching across the Pacific.

In effect, that strategic situation makes the navy and the air force the crucial enabling services in that they will have the responsibility of projecting military power from the continental United States. Yet one must also note that, since those two services can provide control only over air and sea space, which is always fleeting, they cannot provide the control of the ground that politics demands. The holding of ground and the defeating of an opponent will in the end

---

3. At present, with the drawdown in Europe, where the Germans paid a substantial portion of the costs, the army has found itself strained to the breaking point, because it now has to rotate troops through places like Germany and Kuwait to support US strategic aims. That adds immensely to the pressure to soldiers in the states who have to get ready once they return to prepare for the next deployment.

depend on soldiers and marines and the support they provide allies. Moreover, there is the political importance of committing ground forces to the defense of America's allies as well as its interests. It is unrealistic to believe that America's allies will be willing to bear the pain and costs of a ground war without the support of substantial US ground forces.

Interestingly, from the early eighteenth century to the present day, there has been a significant debate in Britain and the United States between those who argued for a blue-water approach to strategy on one hand and a major continental commitment (the support of allies with large ground forces) on the other.[4] In nearly every case those arguing in favor of a commitment to continental allies won out. The result was a series of victories beginning with the War of Spanish Succession (1701–1714) through to the Second World War.[5] Thus, one of the most important calculations American strategists can make will have to do with estimating the size of the ground forces in the continental United States on the basis of the ability of the navy, particularly, and the air force to move the marine corps and the army rapidly in support of allies to troubled spots that lie oceanic distances away.

The defense policy of the Obama administration, such as it is, as well as the refusal of the Republican Congress to articulate a sensible alternative, heightens a number of long-term strategic dangers that

---

4. In the American case, that argument was the line that most isolationists took.

5. For the importance of a commitment of ground forces to America's allies in Europe and Asia, see Williamson Murray, "Grand Strategy, Alliances, and the Anglo-American Way of War," in Williamson Murray and Peter Mansoor, eds., *Grand Strategy and Military Alliances* (Cambridge, 2016).

affect all of the services. The effort to shrink the allocation of resources and funding to the current defense budget reflects the president's efforts to withdraw the United States from much of its global commitments. Ironically, that effort is not all that dissimilar to that of Donald Trump, who, in the midst of his efforts to act like a blowfish, has been articulating a strategic policy for the United States that is for all intents and purposes isolationist. In fact, astonishingly Trump recently commented that "'America first'—the battle cry of the isolationists who attempted to keep the United States out of World War II—will be the major and overriding theme of my administration."[6] By abandoning most of America's alliances from NATO through the Middle East to Asia, Trump would create an isolationist United States that would not require the capabilities to project power to aid America's allies, since it would not have any. But America's influence on the world would rank not much higher than that of Vladimir Putin's Russia, while the Chinese would have free rein throughout not only Southeast Asia, but Asia as well. Nevertheless, one should not single out Trump as the only isolationist among American politicians and media pundits. Isolationism is alive and well throughout the American body politic.

Unfortunately for the long-term strategic prospects of the United States, Obama's defense procurement policies are having the greatest impact on the navy's current commitments. With only 272 ships in service, the navy is being stretched to the breaking point. The current estimate of what it needs to meet its potential commitments suggests 350 ships. Moreover, that estimate rests on current require-

---

6. Quoted in the *New York Times,* 28 April 2016. "America first" was the great theme of the isolationists who attempted to keep the United States out of the Second World War.

ments, not on the navy's long-term needs, given the swelling size of
the Chinese military and naval buildup. The difficulty that confronts
the navy is that even the smallest of its ships and their accompanying
weapons systems require years rather than months to construct.
Moreover, with the limitations on the shipbuilding industry in the
United States—almost entirely confined to the construction of ships
for the navy—only a limited number of shipyards exist to build new
warships. Thus any coherent effort to rebuild the navy to a reasonable level required by America's strategic position is going to take a
considerable period of time, and time may not be available. In the
long term, Obama's unwillingness to fight for reasonable defense
expenditures, particularly in the naval arena, could have a disastrous
effect on America's strategic position in the decade of the 2020s.

Here one should remember what happened in the first years of
the war in the Pacific against the Japanese. On the outbreak of war
on December 7, 1941, the navy's buildup had only begun; as a result
the United States, particularly the navy, took a terrible hammering
from the Japanese from the Battle of the Java Sea to the battles in
the seas around the Solomons and Guadalcanal. As late as September
1942, naval forces were down to a single carrier in the Pacific, and
it was not until the very end of that year that the tables began to turn
in favor of the United States with the arrival of substantial reinforcements, the first wave of the great naval expansion that swamped the
Japanese in 1943 and 1944. The Roosevelt administration had begun
that buildup in 1938, but that effort took more than three years to
reach fruition. It took time to build ships then; and it will take time
in the future.

It is probable that future wars will be come-as-you-are conflicts
that will demand rapid adaptations to conditions unexpected and

unforeseen. They will challenge basic starting assumptions going in. In some respects, if there is substantial downsizing of the American military, such wars will have considerable similarities to British efforts in the Falkland Islands War, which required the hurried, unexpected deployment of the Royal Navy, Royal Air Force, and British Army to an out-of-area location, for which their forces were little prepared.[7] Nevertheless, in spite of a general unpreparedness for such a conflict, the British cobbled together forces that retook the Falklands, though barely.

Finally, US military leaders may well discover that the political leaders have little understanding of what is possible with military means at their disposal or the limitations on the use of force imposed by technology, the influence of the media, or even their own flawed assumptions. The situation may be reminiscent of the conundrum military leaders faced in 1964 and 1965 as President Lyndon Johnson and Defense Secretary Robert McNamara pushed the United States into a war without a long-range strategic framework in the hope that something would turn up. The army's chief of staff, General Harold Johnson, recognized that the proposed entrance into the war in South Vietnam might well last ten years, involve 500,000 US troops, and cost a hundred billion dollars. However, unlike General Matthew Ridgway in 1954, who warned President Dwight Eisenhower of the cost of an intervention in the Vietnam War, General Johnson failed to press his estimate on the president or the secretary of defense.

---

7. The Falklands War of 1982 suggests the intellectual and adaptive qualities that such a war will require. For the best examination of the British side of that conflict, see Max Hastings and Simon Jenkins, *The Battle for the Falklands* (London, 1984).

THE CONSTRAINTS OF STRATEGY

When great crises and wars occur, there may be little time to make coherent judgments, given the unstable context within which wars occur. Here an understanding of potential enemies is crucial to estimating America's strategic situation, because war is an interaction of two or more opponents. As this author noted in the edited volume on *The Making of Strategy,* "statesmen and military leaders live in a world of incomplete information. They do not know in most cases, the strategic intentions and purposes of other powers, except in the most general sense, and their knowledge of their own side is often deficient."[8] Moreover, the larger strategic framework, as a conflict unfolds, alters its shape due to the course of military events and may offer one side or the other unexpected or unforeseen advantages or difficulties.

Here America's intelligence agencies will play a critical role in estimating future opponents; however, as suggested earlier, their record in the past has not been all that effective. Twelve days before ISIS seized Mosul on June 10, 2014, and sent the Iraqi house of cards tumbling down, the president announced at West Point to the graduating second lieutenants that "you are the first class to graduate since 9/11 who may not be sent to combat in Iraq or Afghanistan." Furthermore, while he announced that al Qaeda was largely finished as a serious threat, ISIS did not rate even a mention. (In other circumstances he had described ISIS as a "jayvee team.")[9] There are two

---

8. Williamson Murray and Mark Grimsley, "Introduction: On Strategy," in Williamson Murray, MacGregor Knox, and Alvin Bernstein, *The Making of Strategy: Rulers, States, and War* (Cambridge, 1994), p. 22.

9. Quoted in David Kilcullen, *Blood Year: The Unraveling of Western Counterterrorism* (Oxford, 2016), p. 4.

possibilities that can explain this astonishing miscalculation. On one hand, Obama is a clever politician and, therefore, one can doubt that he would have made such claims had American intelligence informed him that there were troubles ahead in Iraq. Thus the president's comments on the situation in the Middle East before ISIS erupted may represent one more case of a general intelligence failure. On the other hand, it is also possible that the intelligence agencies warned the president and the National Security Council that ISIS represented a major danger in the area and that the president and his advisers entirely ignored the warnings.[10]

It is a lack of understanding of not only the enemy but also of whom the enemy might be that presents the greatest problem to the strategists and political leaders. This is because each nation forms its strategic approach to the world based on a different set of influences. Americans will always find themselves constrained by the need to project military power over continental and oceanic distances; consequently logistical support must be in the forefront of their approach to war. Thus, the influence of geography is paramount for US military forces, just as it represents a significance influence on other nations.[11] Geography has also allowed America's leaders in the period before the two world wars to wait until the last moment before acting. The result was that the allies that America

---

10. In fairness to the CIA, one senior officer received warning from the CIA that ISIS represented a major danger in the region in fall 2011, as he was preparing to testify to Congress.

11. Perceptive and important on this point as usual is Robert D. Kaplan, *The Revenge of Geography: What the Map Tells Us about Coming Conflicts and the Battle against Fate* (New York, 2013).

eventually joined had exhausted the German and Italian enemies before the United States entered the war.

On the other hand, in both world wars it almost led to the dangerous situation of the United States, to quote a colloquial phrase, being a day late and a dollar short. In the First World War, with the US Army totally unprepared for war in Europe by order of President Woodrow Wilson, the Allies came close to losing the war to massive German offensives in spring 1918, before American troops began arriving in substantial numbers.[12] In 1940, only Prime Minister Winston Churchill's dogged, brilliant strategic sense kept Britain in the war long enough for an American polity to enter the conflict, in this case helped by the strategic idiocy of the Japanese and Germans, the former in attacking Pearl Harbor and the latter in declaring war on the United States, when there was no need to do so.[13]

Similarly, geography has been paramount for the Germans but in a very different fashion. In the center of Europe, whether they have possessed a strong military power, as during the two world wars, or a weak military power as during the Thirty Years' War, the Germans have found themselves in a conflict on or near their own territory. Thus, logistics has been far down in their list of

---

12. For the German offensives in spring 1918, see David T. Zabecki, *The German 1918 Offensives: A Case Study in the Operational Level of War* (London, 2006).

13. Adolf Hitler's declaration of war on the United States was enthusiastically supported by the Kriegsmarine, while the Luftwaffe and army failed to raise any objections. The German decision to declare war on the United States reflected a belief that Germany's defeat in 1918 was the result of the Jews and Communists stabbing an unbeaten army in the back and that the arrival of 2,000,000 US troops in Europe played only a little role in that defeat.

priorities.[14] Yet perhaps even more damaging to the Reich's position in the two world wars was the general ignorance and contempt German leaders had for their opponents, particularly the Americans and the Russians.

For the Russians, the great distances of that nation have provided little of the security that distance has provided the United States, because Russian distances have been land-based. In the end, Russia has won its wars only because its invaders have exhausted themselves in tearing up the landscape. The result has given Russian leaders an approach to strategy resting on paranoia about their nation's security needs. The larger political weakness that the Soviet leadership possessed was inherent in the nature of their ideology: a set of beliefs that prevented them from understanding the flexibility and imagination that characterized the American economy. It was thus inconceivable to them that the American capitalist economy— as well as the capitalist economies of its allies—would outperform their own efforts to accomplish what Josef Stalin lugubriously called the Soviet effort to build up "socialism in one state." Nevertheless, whatever its differences with the Soviet regime, the current leadership in the Kremlin possesses a paranoia similar to that which marked the Soviet leadership throughout much of the Cold War.

Adding to the complexity of strategic decision making factors such as the historical baggage and myths that nations carry, the political nature of their regimes, as well as the economic strength of their polity, all exercise crucial influences on the making of strategy. But perhaps the most important factor is the nature of the state's leader-

---

14. The German invasion of the Soviet Union in June 1941 is the best example of how extraordinarily sloppy the Germans were in their logistical planning.

ship. Germany's terrifying rise in the late 1930s and early 1940s and its disastrous collapse during the course of the Second World War are simply unimaginable without the baleful leadership that Adolf Hitler provided the Reich. Of equal importance to the war's outcome was that, over the course of the first 100 days of his period as prime minister, from May through August 1940, Churchill provided stunning leadership and oratory that motivated the British people. His leadership thwarted the appeasers who wanted to make peace with the seemingly victorious Reich, gave the British people the sense that their country must stay the course in fighting Nazi Germany whatever the odds, ruthlessly removed the threat of the French Navy with the Royal Navy's attack on the French fleet at Mers-el-Kébir, and made the crucial steps toward a partnership with the United States and its president, Franklin Roosevelt.

Thus, in every respect the rational actor model so beloved by American political scientists is utter nonsense. Had such a model existed in Germany in 1943, the Germans would have surrendered at that point; had such a model existed in Britain in June 1940, the British also would have quit before the Battle of Britain. As Clausewitz points out, theory "must also take the human factor into account and find room for courage, boldness, even foolhardiness. The art of war deals with living and moral forces."[15] Clausewitz also noted that theory—in his terms military theory, but we might extend his definition to include international relations theory—must be "an analytic investigation leading to a close *acquaintance* with the subject; applied to experience—in our case, to . . . [international relations] it leads to a thorough *familiarity* with it."[16]

---

15. Clausewitz, *On War*, p. 86.
16. Ibid., p. 141.

What is clear is that the American statesmen who guided the nation from 1940 to the end of the Cold War understood Sun Tzu's "other" far better than the enemies of the nation did. As they did in the past, personalities will drive strategic decision making in the United States as well as among its allies and enemies. Here, the United States has been lucky in the leaders responsible for guiding its strategy in its war. Lincoln and Roosevelt were particularly effective leaders in the Civil War and the Second World War, while Truman, Eisenhower, and Reagan all stand out for their leadership during the long decades of the Cold War.

In the end, it will be strategic wisdom and leadership that will determine how the United States and its military forces will perform in the coming decades of the twenty-first century if the nation is to navigate the inherent shoals of a dangerous world.[17] Here lies the great conundrum, because, as this book has suggested so far, there is little in the education of the elites who run this nation presently or for the future or much of the military leadership to suggest that the strategic wisdom that guided the United States in the Second World War and much of the Cold War will be available to meet the unexpected strategic challenges of the future.[18]

In terms of judging American strategy in the two world wars and the Cold War, US strategic wisdom stands up far better than

---

17. Both strategic wisdom and leadership are necessary, because Churchill provided plenty of wisdom throughout the 1930s, but the British people offered him no chance to exercise leadership until May 10, 1940, when the game was almost up.

18. Colin Gray is fond of saying that the future is not foreseeable, and for the most part he is right. In this case the future is foreseeable, given the wreckage that American academics have made of the study of history, literature, and geography (the latter no longer taught).

its opponents in those three conflicts. Yet, one should not forget that it reflected more emphasis on history and literature in the education of the leaders who developed and executed American strategy from 1940 through to the end of the Cold War. It also reflected the fact that our opponents had no realistic sense of the economic and military power of the United States. Given our performance over the past several decades, will the current educational system provide American leaders with a similar degree of political and strategic sophistication, or can they rely on those powers which oppose us to possess similar flawed assumptions and ignorant calculations about the nature and extent of American power?

How one creates and exercises strategic leadership depends greatly on the individual statesman, because the international situation is always in flux. After he had left office as chancellor and entered the period of forced retirement, Bismarck remarked:

> As long as he lives the statesman is always unprepared. In the attainment of that for which he strives he is too dependent on the participation of others, a fluctuating and incalculable factor. . . . Even after the greatest success he cannot say with certainty, "Now it is achieved; I am done with it," and look back with complacency at what has been accomplished.[19]

As for the potential for war, one can make some guesses, but they represent reality no more than predictions as to what NFL team is

---

19. Quoted by Marcus Jones, "Bismarckian Strategic Policy," in Williamson Murray and Richard Hart Sinnreich, *Successful Strategies: Triumphing in War and Peace from Antiquity to the Present* (Cambridge, 2013), p. 239.

going to win the Super Bowl in 2020. The rapidly improving capabilities of the computer and communication revolutions are not only driving enormous changes in the interactions of individual human beings but affecting the political landscape. At the same time those revolutions have profound implications for military institutions and the conduct of war. In particular, the technological and computer revolutions are developing a whole host of new and deadly weapons.

But how these terrifying new weapons will interact on the battlefield is impossible to predict, particularly at the high end, where the conflicting powers will have similar capabilities in the cyber and communications domains. Given the experience of the twentieth century, the most unlikely conflict would be one between the two superpowers, because of the possibility of such a conflict going nuclear. But that does not eliminate the considerable possibility of the two superpowers waging proxy wars. At least in such cases the ideological factor of the free world versus the communist world, which made the Cold War so dangerous, would not be present.

Nevertheless, the potential of "small wars"—driven by the Sunni-Shi'a divide in the Middle East or a major blowup between India and Pakistan—to inflict significant damage on portions of the global landscape is immense. Moreover, the West is seeing immediately before its eyes in Syria and Iraq the wreckage being caused by a terrible religious/civil war to which it has been willing to react only minimally. The resulting massive flow of refugees from the Middle East is already upsetting Europe's demographic and political balance in what have been presumed to be stable states. Continuing waves of such migrants, coming from entirely different cultures and some bearing the seeds of religious fanaticism, present the possibility of expanding terrorist activities. These will magnify the swelling anger of those still in the majority, who believe they have some claim to and belief in a religious and cultural heritage that the elite intellectuals in their society have so disdainfully discarded. It is indeed a brew of anger and bitterness that would delight Macbeth's three witches.

THE SEARCH FOR PRECISION AND THE ACHILLES' HEEL OF TECHNOLOGY

Over the past half century, American political and military leaders have attempted to make war less costly in human terms. In terms of lowering American casualties in combat, that is a wholly worthwhile endeavor.[20] But that effort has carried over into the creation of unrealistic rules of engagement governing the use of weapons and representing efforts to reduce civilian casualties. To a certain extent, this has driven the revolution in precision munitions. In the Gulf War of 1991, extensive interviews with Iraqi prisoners of war indicated that the coalition aircraft they most feared was the ancient—even at that time—B-52. Above all, they emphasized the terrifying shock that strikes carried out miles away had on their perspective of the war and morale.[21]

---

20. That effort has also led to some truly bizarre conclusions by supposed moralists who have clearly never studied war, much less been involved in the bloody business. In the aftermath of the Gulf War in 1991 there were some commentators who argued that the low number of casualties suffered by US and coalition forces in comparison to the high number suffered by the Iraqi military somehow represented a moral failing on the basis of proportionality.

21. For air operations during the Gulf War, see Williamson Murray, "Operations," report 1, vol. 2, in Eliot Cohen, ed., *The Gulf War Air Power Survey* (Washington, DC, 1993).

Ironically, because the B-52 computers were misaligned, the heavy bombers never hit their targets at which they were aiming. It did not matter, because the impact of the B-52 strikes was largely on the morale of Iraqi soldiers hunkered down in the deserts of Kuwait and southern Iraq. The horrendous noise and shaking of the earth from strikes even a dozen miles distant affected them deeply. Ironically, in the bombing of ISIS, including its military forces and encampments in the desert, US military and political leaders have not been willing to use the B-52. The reason behind this unwillingness lies in a belief among the political leadership in Washington that precision strikes prevent all collateral damage, which they do not. Such beliefs entirely miss the purpose of the use of military force and air power in particular, which is to wreck the enemy's morale as much as to achieve physical damage and kill his soldiers.

The emphasis on technology is not surprising, given that it has been one of the strengths of American society for more than a century. Yet, there are limits to what technology can achieve by itself, while the enemy will always get a vote, and the more sophisticated and competent he is, the more likely that he will seek out and discover means to disrupt and distort our technological capabilities. In the conflicts that spun out of the global war on terrorism, the United States has enjoyed a massive superiority in weapons and the technology of those systems over the capabilities of its opponents. Nevertheless, one should not forget that even with the Americans' technological superiority, the ragged guerrillas of al Qaeda in Iraq and the Taliban in Afghanistan have caused US and coalition ground forces no end of trouble since 2003.

As suggested in the second chapter, the world is going through a technological and scientific revolution that in every respect rivals the great "military-social revolutions" of the past. But unlike the period from 1914 through 1990, where the military organizations were the primary drivers behind revolutionary changes in technology, the current period looks quite similar to the period before 1914, when factors outside the military were largely responsible for the technological revolution. The point here is that the technological changes occurring during the past three decades will make military adaptation to the complexities of combat with sophisticated opponents even more difficult for armies, navies, and air forces than was the case in the First World War. The result of that murderous process of adaptation on the Western Front to the technological and scientific changes of the period before the First World War was a bloodbath that destroyed the comfortable assumptions on which European and American progress rested.

The impact of the computer-driven, technological revolution on military capabilities and future potential has certainly become clear over the past quarter of a century. The British military thinker and professor Christopher Coker has noted the following about the rapid pace of technological development in military capabilities over the past two decades:

> It is the "intelligence" gained from sensors that allows artillery to be integrated into a "system" that permits co-ordinated fire from a multiplicity of platforms, such as attack helicopters and Unmanned Aerial Vehicles, and the intelligence of some of these systems is already impressive. Take the Smart-155, a projectile which releases two sensor-fused sub-munitions from the shell case in mid-flight. Each can identify targets by size and their 3-D heat signatures (in other words, each can choose other targets if

the initial one is found to be on fire). And with the introduction quite soon of 3-D mapping, an observer will be able to pinpoint the exact location of a target on a 3-D map and share it with the shooter. Soon artificial intelligence in command and control systems will come on-stream and allow the next generation of projectiles not only to identify targets but even to prioritize "kills." In the not-too-distant future, they will be able to determine autonomously whether to fire or not.[22]

At present, through the efforts of its scientists and technologists, the Defense Advanced Research Projects Agency (DARPA) is pushing the envelope for the development of new weapons in a fashion that is unusual in the federal bureaucracy, particularly in an agency active since the 1950s.[23] Clearly unmanned aerial vehicles (UAVs) are already a game changer at every level, from marine corps and army infantry platoons to potential future fighter aircraft. The ability to hit terrorist targets virtually anywhere in the world from UAVs controlled from Nevada has enabled the United States to wage a war on terrorists that puts no one in danger except for the collateral victims. It is likely that the F-35 will be the last manned fighter produced by the United States to be replaced by pilotless aircraft. Unmanned robots will play a larger and larger role in ground war. Hypersonic missiles are at present being tested by the United States, Russia, and China. Traveling at the speed of Mach 10

---

22. Christopher Coker, *Future War* (Malden, MA, 2015), p. 83.

23. Most of DARPA's work remains highly classified, but enough leaks suggest that the advances in weaponry are truly terrifying, even for those who lived through the thermonuclear times of the Cold War.

or more, such missiles will make a defensive response almost impossible, given the time between detection and arrival on target.

But there are several caveats worth underlining. The first is that much of the advances in weaponry are largely targeted at the potential of high-end conflict against opponents who have capabilities—such as the Chinese—which are approaching those of the United States. Such opponents will also possess nuclear weapons and the reality is that, as with the standoff with the Soviet Union during the Cold War, improved conventional weapons will serve in the framework of deterrence. Thus, such weapons may never find themselves used in the fashion for which they have been designed. Improvements in missiles, UAVs, and aircraft carrying nuclear weapons will hopefully make deterrence work among the major powers in the coming decades as it did during the Cold War.

At present and for at least a decade, if current funding levels remain in place, the United States will enjoy a significant measure of military superiority over its potential opponents. Admittedly, a war with China would prove immensely costly for both sides, but in the end the Chinese would lose badly. But, given the Chinese buildup, a potential American victory may not be the case in another decade, unless there is a significant investment in American forces in the near future. Such an effort will require the far-sighted wisdom of the American people as well as their leaders, much like the Athenians and their leader Themistocles in the 480s BC.

One of the incalculables in thinking about future wars lies in the technological systems that midrank powers or groups such as ISIS might gain in the future. The most frightening would be the possession of a nuclear weapon by groups that have no sense of responsibility for the long-term effects of detonating such weapons. That, of course, is why the collapse of Pakistan into a failed state would have such dangerous consequences for the world. Moreover, a war between Pakistan and India would carry with it the dangerous possibility that it might go nuclear, which would create a humanitarian crisis of unbelievable proportions, while the fallout would pose a global threat.

Although the US military enjoys extraordinary advantages at present, there are danger signs. The service forces and their capabilities rest on a robust communications network as well as cyber and electronic systems. Especially important are the space-based systems for a vast array of intelligence functions, communications, the accuracy of munitions, targeting, and even the movement of US combat vehicles on the battlefield. As one army officer noted to the author, "we can't (and won't) go to war without SATCOM, GPS, or space-based imagery." The army and the marines, supposedly the least sophisticated of the services, underline how dependent the American military has become on technology. As one briefing recently noted, the army has evolved over the past decade "from a space-enabled Army to a *fully space-dependent Army*." It added that, in fact, virtually everything involving US military operations relies on links to and through space-based systems. Just a small listing of the army support systems that depend on space suggests the extent of that dependency: GPS (Global Positioning System), SATCOM (satellite communication), RISTA (reconnaissance, surveillance, and target acquisition), SIGINT (signals intelligence), electronic sensors, JDAM (joint direct attack munition), Excalibur (155 mm extended-range artillery), and GPS-guided MLRS, for example. Simply put, the ground forces of the United States are dependent on technological and space-based systems to execute their most basic tasks on the battlefield. This is also true to an even greater extent for navy and air force.

There are difficulties. Again, to quote an army official: "capabilities create dependencies, and dependencies create vulnerabilities." The problem is that both computer-based systems and space-based systems are vulnerable to being hacked by an enemy. Fred Kaplan, a national security reporter, recently noted the following on the current vulnerability of the defense department's sophisticated communications network: "In several recent exercises and war games that [a defense science board] reviewed, Red Teams, using exploits that any skilled hacker could download from the Internet, 'invariably' penetrated the Defense Department's networks, 'disrupting or completely beating' the Blue Team."[24]

What makes this so astonishing is that in 1997 the National Security Agency's Red Team in an exercise with the title of ELIGIBLE RECEIVER basically broke into every system the department of defense possessed. Only one marine officer during that exercise recognized that something was wrong and disconnected his system. One would have thought that in the intervening period of nearly two decades, there would have been significant improvement in the defense department and the services' ability to protect their communication and computer systems from hackers or simply their own incompetence. But then it is well to remember how easily Snowden downloaded the masses of highly classified material which he then uploaded to the Internet. In his case, it was largely the result of gross

---

24. Fred Kaplan, *Dark Territory: The Secret History of Cyber War* (New York, 2016), p. 275.

security breaches made by the contracting firms working for the National Security Agency.

This author remembers a briefing he received from a British Army brigadier in 2000 that examined the nature of special operations forces thirty years into the future.[25] The officer posited that 70 percent of the force would look much as it did in the past. However, the other 30 percent would look very different. It would include women, because they could go places where men could not, particularly in the Middle East. But the key new group in British special forces would be twenty years old or younger, who would hardly fit into the military culture of the Special Air Service and the Special Boat Service, but who would possess extraordinary capabilities as hackers.[26] There lies the problem with the hierarchical nature of the American military and the nation's intelligence agencies. One can hardly imagine the use of such individuals or a willingness to reach

---

25. The fact that *one* British brigadier was charged by the British Army's leadership to examine the problem of future forces suggests a great deal about the difference between the British military and the US military. In the latter case, undoubtedly twenty staff officers and colonels would have addressed the problem and would have come up with a massive briefing but no coherent argument or examination of the problem. Moreover, the fact that the brigadier reached out to a foreign academic is noteworthy. In the American case, no one in such a study would have reached out to an American academic, much less a foreign academic, given the high-level security classification involved in thinking about the future. And, of course, that is why the Team B of academics in the late 1970s came up with a far more realistic appraisal of Soviet aims and capabilities than did the supposed experts in the CIA.

26. Here the British experiences in the Second World War are worth noting. F. H. Hinsley, after the war a major historian, found himself recruited into Bletchley Park in early September 1939 because of his fluency in German. By the end of 1940, he had become one of the most important analysts in British intelligence, and in March 1941 he would play a key role in breaking into the U-boat Enigma cyphers.

out to them or, for that matter, other subject matter experts in most of the intelligence community. Admittedly, this author may be entirely wrong in that supposition, but the continued inability of America's intelligence agencies and military organizations to close the gaps in its cypher systems suggests deeply troubling bureaucratic malaise in the system, one that refuses to judge individuals by competence rather than by age and seniority.

What is clear is that America's opponents in future wars will also target the extensive space-based communications systems upon which the American military depends for the conduct of its global operations. The simplest approach to disrupting the satellites on which those systems depend would be to explode a relatively low-yield nuclear device in lower orbit. The resulting electromagnetic pulse (emp) would be sufficient to render useless virtually all the satellites in low orbit. It is unlikely that either the United States or China would explode such a weapon, because it would take out friendly systems as well as those of an enemy. Moreover, since none of the commercial satellites on which the Internet, civilian communications, television transmissions, among other commercial usages, are protected from an emp burst, the result would be catastrophic to the global economy on which both the United States and China depend. The effects caused by the frying of commercial satellites would considerably affect the military side as well. For example, Central Command depends on commercial satellites for more than three-quarters of its bandwidth.[27]

---

27. In an unclassified conference in Washington, representatives of the defense department's communications system tried to persuade the commercial providers to protect their satellites, which means shielding them with lead. Their reply was that to do so would be so expensive that it would be cheaper simply to replace the satellites.

If neither the Chinese nor the Americans are likely to explode a nuclear weapon in space, because of the damage it would cause to their own satellites, the same cannot be said for the North Koreans or the Pakistanis. One can well imagine a North Korea on the brink of collapse or confronted with American and Chinese major economic pressure taking the risks of such a move as a means to preserve the regime without the risks of actually killing people. The damage to a global economy dependent on communications systems for transferring funds and information can well be imagined. Would the United States and its South Korean allies actually risk war in response to a nuclear-armed North Korea? Doubtful.

If the Chinese would be unwilling to attack the US satellite system by exploding a nuclear weapon in space, they have already proven to have other means at their disposal: namely, antisatellite missiles aimed at taking out particular satellites that are in orbit. Such an effort would have a long-term impact on the Chinese as well, because the number of antisatellite attacks in a wartime effort to take out US systems would so clutter up lower orbits with smashed-up satellites that they would make further use of space virtually impossible. The larger point is that the American military had better be prepared in future conflicts in which it finds itself to operate with a significant portion of its capabilities degraded. Any war between sophisticated powers will, to a considerable extent, take part in the dark. And that raises the worrisome question as to how effective US weapons will prove in the event an opponent is able to degrade severely their capabilities. Similarly, how effective will American fighting forces be when the communication links fail, when commanders on the sharp end have to make decisions on their own, and when GPS no longer provides accurate readings or any readings at all?

CONCLUSION

There is no way to forecast the future. There are no silver bullets in the business of war. As suggested earlier, the military profession is not only the most demanding physically; it is also the most demanding intellectually. We policy makers, politicians, senior military leaders, and scholars all worry about what nation or group the United States military will fight and where we will fight. But in the end we cannot know. Perhaps we need to focus more realistically on how we will fight and how we prepare to fight. And that demands serious thinking about the art of war.

APPENDIX

POTENTIAL TROUBLE SPOTS

THERE ARE OBVIOUS TROUBLE SPOTS THROUGHOUT THE WORLD. They all have the potential to explode into serious conflicts at any time in the immediate or distant future. Whether they do or not, as the above chapters have suggested, depends on factors that no one can predict. Thus, we have left their discussion out of the main argument. Instead they now appear in this appendix for the reader to peruse. Above all, they are meant to be suggestive rather than predictive and as a means only to indicate possible dangers that might lie ahead.

In the early 1990s Samuel Huntington, the great Harvard political scientist, published an article in *Foreign Affairs* titled "The Clash of Civilizations." That seminal piece of imaginative strategic writing met with howls of outrage from much of the West's academic and political world. Several years later the professor published a somewhat milder version of his argument in book form, which again received considerable criticism from those who believed that matters in the world were largely on the upswing now that the Cold War had ended in the triumph of the West over the Soviet Union.

Instead with democracy and neoliberal economic competition leading the way, the world was supposedly heading into an unparalleled
period of peace and prosperity.

How far away those hopes and dreams appear a quarter of a
century later. Instead, there are now a growing number of trouble
spots, for which the United States seems singularly unprepared to
confront, while a number of major powers are now challenging the
United States not only politically, but militarily as well. Some of
those challenges represent straight old-fashioned power politics,
while others remain deeply embedded in the culture and religions
of peoples "of whom we know nothing."

THE MIDDLE EAST

The great Middle Eastern expert Bernard Lewis, now in the second
century of his life, noted in 2011 the following about the Arab
world:

> For the first time in almost 200 years, the rulers and to some
> extent the peoples of the Middle East are having to accept final
> responsibility for their own affairs; to recognize their own mis-
> takes and accept the consequences. This was difficult to internal-
> ize, even to perceive, after so long a period. For the entire
> lifetimes of those who formulate and conduct policy at the pres-
> ent time and of their predecessors for many generations, the vital
> decisions were made elsewhere, ultimate control lay elsewhere,
> and the principle task of statesmanship and diplomacy was as far
> as possible to avoid or reduce the dangers of this situation and to

exploit such opportunities as it might from time to time offer. It is very difficult to forsake the habits not just of a lifetime but of a whole era of history. The difficulty is that much greater when alien cultural, social and economic preeminence continues and even increases, despite the ending of political and military domination.[1]

The great problem hanging over the Arab world lies not just in the myriad immediate conflicts confronting it, but also in the all-encompassing shadow that the rise of the West over the past five centuries has cast. It took the Europeans and those who have accepted much of the West's civilization over five centuries to create what has some resemblance to an equitable society. Nevertheless, it is worth pointing out that the conduct of war has hardly been absent from the onrush of Western civilization. After all, the Europeans, the Americans, and the Japanese managed to lapse into two horrific world wars in the first half of the twentieth century, wars that came close to destroying nearly all of their civil, intellectual, and political accomplishments and capital.

On the other hand, the Islamic world, particularly its Arab portion, has found itself and its deeply held beliefs pitched into the modern world at the beginning of the twentieth century with none of the turns and intellectual conflicts that marked much of the history of the West. Today the greater Arab world that stretches from Morocco to Mesopotamia confronts the stark choice of either adapting to or escaping from the world of globalization created by societies

---

1. Bernard Lewis, *The End of Modern History in the Middle East* (Stanford, CA, 2011), p. 5.

and political entities that are foreign in every sense of the word to its culture and politics. As with all societies, there is a wide variety of opinions among the Arabs themselves, among those whom we might call modernizers, those looking for radical change, and conservatives—the latter largely religious in nature and motivated by a desire to hold onto their interpretation of what they regard as the fundamental truths of twelfth-century Islam. Sprinkled throughout that world are violently religious and fundamentalist "true" believers and groups.

More often than not led by corrupt, authoritarian regimes, addicted to the export of petroleum products, which have offered little incentive for industrialization or modernization, and burdened by cultural or ideological obstacles to education, especially of women, much of the Arab-Islamic world has fallen steadily behind the developed world. The rage of radical Islamists feeds off the lies of their corrupt leaders, the rhetoric of radical and irresponsible imams, the falsification of their own media, and resentment at a Western world that has dominated so much of their history over the past century. If tensions between the Arab world's past and present were not enough, across the heartland lie deep and often violent tribal, religious, and political divisions. For the most part, one cannot speak of a national identity, although there are some exceptions. Egypt, Tunisia, and Morocco, in particular, do represent exceptions. Nevertheless, at best the Arab world shares a religious identity of Islam, but one increasingly splintered between Sunni and Shi'a.

Not surprisingly, political instability throughout the region is inevitable. But the difficulties extend beyond inter-Arab religious and tribal difficulties. The narrative of the Arab world begins in the seventh century with the explosion of the religious believers from the Arabian Peninsula. Within a few decades the invaders had incorporated the entire southern and eastern shores of the Mediterranean into their new world. For the next five centuries the Arab-Islamic world represented one of the world's greatest civilizations, while the quarreling nascent tribal entities of Europe barely maintained their independence. However, in the thirteenth century the disaster of the Mongol invasion of the Middle East and the sack of Baghdad, accompanied by the rise of the Turks, ended Arab political domination of Islam.[2]

For the most part, the Arab world has yet to adapt to the political challenges raised by the modern world; its various segments remain tied to tribe, clan, and family rather than to any conception of the state. Without the overriding powers that modernizing states possesses, such as those that ended the bitter contest among Catholics and Protestants in seventeenth-century Europe, there is the possibility that the Sunni-Shi'a contest may explode into a ferocious religious conflict involving Iran and its Shi'a proxies on one side to the north and east of the Persian Gulf and the Sunni groupings lying to the south and west.

But it is not the Arab world that presents the only threat or even the greatest danger in terms of the troubles that it might cause to the external world. After all, at present none of the regional powers possesses nuclear weapons, although that may change in the future, if the Iranians disregard the agreements they made with the Obama administration and others. Nevertheless, if the possibilities in other

---

2. Saddam once argued that the Mongols had sacked Baghdad because the Jews had persuaded them to turn south into Mesopotamia rather than continue their rampage into Western Europe.

parts of the world seem less likely than a disastrous conflict in the Middle East, one cannot ignore the potential for miscalculations elsewhere, especially in a world driven not by comfortable trends and rational actors, but rather by chance, accident, mistaken calculations, and above all by human fallibilities, genius, and incompetence. Thus, other troubling spots deserve equal attention with the difficulties of the Middle East. And one must not forget that wars, such as the Falklands War of spring 1982, may spring out of what may appear to bystanders as the most obtuse and obscure of causes.

THE RUSSIAN PROBLEM

Toward the end of his life in the late 1960s, Charles de Gaulle prophesied that the Soviet Union would collapse before the century had ended and that the resulting Russian state would find itself with the Urals as its eastern frontier within another century. In the first case he was obviously correct; the second prophesy remains open, but in terms of the strategic sophistication of the current cabal running the heartland of the former Soviet Union, it does not appear all that far-fetched. From the outside, the successors to the Soviet Union appear to have created a political entity residing somewhere between thuggery and kleptocracy. Certainly the poisoning of Alexander Litvinenko with polonium-210 by Russian FSB operatives, one of whom is now serving in the Duma, underlines the nature of the regime as well as its inheritance of the murderous ways of the Soviet Union's secret police, the KGB.[3]

---

3. The FSB is the successor to the KGB.

Nevertheless, to understand the Russians and the current regime, one needs to recognize the deep-seated paranoia that marks a nation that over the course of its history has suffered a series of devastating invasions. In the thirteenth century the Mongols ravaged Kievan Russia, destroying a polity already on a par with Europe's medieval kingdoms in terms of its civilization.[4] An invasion by the Poles followed in the seventeenth century, the Swedes in the eighteenth century, Napoleon in the nineteenth century, and the Germans twice in the twentieth century. The last of those invasions, which began with Operation Barbarossa in June 1941, saw the German invaders kill 7,000,000 Soviet soldiers and in excess of 20,000,000 civilians.

Thus, Russians in general, and not just Vladimir Putin, have viewed NATO's eastward advances as aggressive; not surprisingly, they responded similarly to Georgian approaches to NATO as well as to the collapse of the corrupt puppet regime they were supporting in the Ukraine. Finally, one should not discount the real troubles the Russians confront in the Caucasus, the Chechens being only the most obvious nationality among a group of mountaineering people with centuries long hatreds fueling the discord in the region. Given the Russians' distrust of the warring tribes and putative states in the Caucasus, it is not surprising that they reacted so strongly against Georgia, considering the talk that that insignificant state might join NATO.

To a certain extent the Russians have recovered from the disastrous collapse of the Soviet Union and their hegemony which stretched deep

---

4. Significantly, it was during the same period that the Mongols ravaged Mesopotamia and left as a memorial to their Weltanschauung a vast pyramid of skulls of those they had slaughtered. Arab civilization never fully recovered with the Turks assuming the leadership of the Islamic world.

into Central Europe. But the economic recovery has rested almost entirely on the boom in oil and gas prices, which gave the Russians not only massive amounts of cash, but political influence as well. Unfortunately for the Russian people, however, much of that cash has ended up in the pockets of Putin and his inner circle, while desperately needed infrastructure projects, such as repairs to the railroad system, construction of highways and bridges, as well as a minimal investment in a road network among Russia's European cities, have yet to materialize. Thus, in economic terms, the regime's leaders are praying for a return of high energy prices to provide sufficient resources to keep the Russian people relatively happy.

There is, however, little chance that this regime will spend any upturn in energy prices in creating the industrial base that might make Russia competitive in world markets. Ironically, current economic troubles seem to be having little impact on popular attitudes toward the regime, mostly because the Russian people expect a hostile external world and thus, have simply hunkered down to ride out the storm—after all there have been worse storms in Russian history. Adding to the litany of trouble confronting Russia is a collapse in the birth rate that, combined with the falling life expectancy of Russian males, indicates demographic troubles of the first order.

In military terms, the Russians dominate their neighbors, and their use of military force against the Chechens, Georgians, and Ukrainians has underlined the genuine threat that Putin's regime represents to the neighborhood. Moreover, substantial Russian spending on defense, almost entirely due to the largesse of high oil prices, has provided the sharp end of the nation's military forces with an impressive array of weaponry and well-trained troops, especially airborne and special forces. But there are limits to what the Russians can achieve with their military power. Putin pulled his forces out of Syria in a relatively short time not so much because the regime could not continue to support them financially, but mainly because in the largest sense the Russian military are reminiscent of a Potemkin village, with the conscript forces behind an impressive façade, the former largely reflective of the ill-trained, alcoholic conscripts of the Red Army. In any case, the conscripts serve for a single year, hardly sufficient time to achieve any degree of military effectiveness.

Against the ineffective militaries of the Caucasus, the Ukraine, Belarus, or Central Asia the Russians would have little difficulty in any conflict. Against NATO forces they would struggle. It is not so much that the Russians would not enjoy immediate success in a war against the Baltic Republics and their NATO supporters, for example, because they would, should they employ direct military force. But what has worked in the Crimea has had a disastrous impact on the rest of the Ukraine. In effect it has turned even those living in the central and eastern Ukraine into Ukrainian nationalists. Thus, Putin's aggressive actions, although popular in Russia, carry with them the danger of the Russians losing control of their surrounding neighborhood.

Moreover, in countries where law and order have emerged the Russians would have considerable difficulty in stirring up trouble. The possibility of using hybrid warfare is not in the cards to Russia's west. Against the Poles the Russians would run into real difficulty. That is probably why several of the more recent war games the Russian general staff has run have ended with the use of nuclear weapons against NATO. Most likely the outcomes of these war games are an indication of Russia's military weakness rather than strength. Nevertheless, America's feckless foreign policy under the current administration has encouraged Putin to take risks, given his contempt for Obama. As he is reputed to have commented, the foreign policy of the American president seems aimed at "creating socialism in one country."

In the long term, the greatest threat to Russia is the rise of China and its military and economic power. As the Russians supply China with energy and weapons even as the growth and strategic profile of its neighbor to the southeast outstrips them in every category of power, the Kremlin faces the grim likelihood of becoming a diminishing junior partner in an anti-Western coalition dominated by Beijing, which has never renounced its claim to the vast areas of Siberia. Given significant Chinese investments in that area over the past several decades, it is only a matter of time before Beijing raises its ancient claims to much of Siberia, claims which possess far more legitimacy than China's claims on the South China Sea. Moreover, a steady flow of migrant farmers from China's poorer areas, who are eager to work rather than drink, is slowly changing the population balance in Siberia's border areas with Manchuria.

But Putin and his cronies are clever men, rather than wise men, and tweaking the nose of the United States is far more fun than facing up to the real strategic and political problems their nation confronts. Their willingness to meddle in the affairs of their neighbors also carries with it the distinct danger that what they regard as a limited military action could spiral out of control. This is especially true in the Baltic. While the Germans and French would be less than enthusiastic about coming to the aid of Estonia, for example, that is certainly not the case with the Poles. But in the long term, their playing with China entirely ignores de Gaulle's perceptive warning.

THE CHINESE-ASIAN PROBLEM

The historical baggage that China carries in substance is quite different from that of Russia. Nevertheless, like the Russians, the Chinese have confronted innumerable invasions that have shaken the nation to its roots. In the Second World War, the Japanese looted, murdered, and raped their way across much of China, but, as has been the case throughout Chinese history, the Chinese hunkered down and survived. However, two other events in the twentieth century may have left an even deeper impression on the Chinese and their leaders: the humiliation over the collapse of the Manchu Empire at the beginning of the century with the resulting scramble by the European powers to achieve treaty rights from the wreckage.

Equally damaging to China and its people was the rule of Mao Tse-tung, who not only imposed a bloody purge on the peasants after the traumas of the war against the Japanese invaders, but then introduced efforts to drag China into the twentieth century with the Great Leap Forward and the Cultural Revolution, which killed tens of millions. In the end Mao, perhaps due to his longevity, may well have won the trophy as the most murderous ruler in the twentieth century, which is no mean achievement given the competition.

Perhaps the heaviest baggage the Chinese carry is a sense of entitlement from their history having lasted several millennia. The contrast with the West could not be more graphic. To most in the West, the Greeks and the Romans are little more than the tired myths of the past with little connection to the present. Few, if any, of the graduates of America's elite colleges and universities have read, much less studied, Greek tragedy. This stands in stark contrast to China, where even after Mao's massive efforts to break with the country's history, memory and a connection to the national past remain deeply embedded in the thinking of not only the elites but the general public as well. The fact that many of China's current strategic debates find themselves resting on the arguments in texts written in the period well before Christ suggest how deeply that culture is embedded within the society. The result is a belief among most Chinese that China deserves its rightful place as *the* great power, as opposed to one of the great powers. Thus, they see period of the nineteenth century through most of the twentieth century as one of terrible humiliation—a period, nevertheless, similar to other dark periods in Chinese history. But significantly to most Chinese, China is regaining its rightful place as *the* great power.

China's spectacular economic revival over the course of almost four decades has vaulted it into the extraordinary position of being able to challenge politically and militarily the United States in East and South Asia. The Chinese military buildup has already placed US forces in Southeast Asia at risk, given the upsurge in the People's Liberation Army's (PLA) increasing technological sophistication. Yet, there is irony in the increasing aggressiveness the Chinese have displayed, policies largely based on the PLA's military strength. A decade ago, there was considerable debate within China about the historical parallels of the emergence of great powers in a global context during previous centuries. Chinese commentators took considerable note of the fate of Wilhelmine Germany, which by its arrogant and threatening behavior had basically solidified a great coalition against it and ensured its eventual defeat in the First World War.

That sense that German actions and aggressiveness in the first half of the twentieth century carry a warning of significance to China appears to have disappeared from strategic discussions in Chinese media and academia. Instead, an increasingly aggressive military posture has taken its place. Certainly, China's moves in South and Southeast Asia suggest an extraordinary arrogance, even by American standards. In an area to which the Chinese have no legitimate claim, namely the Spratly Islands, their military are well along toward construction of an artificial island base, from which, at least according to James Clapper, director of US National Intelligence, they will be able "to project military capabilities in the South China Sea beyond that which is required for point defense of [their] outposts."

The result, not surprisingly, has been a closing of ranks among China's neighbors, as the smaller nations of Southeast Asia draw closer to the United States. In effect, the Chinese have presented the United States with allies eager to cooperate with the Americans against the Chinese threat. Perhaps the most astonishing is that the Vietnamese, against whom the United States waged a ferocious war fifty years ago, have become an ally of the United States for all intents and purposes.[5] The difficulty for the United States is that unlike Europe, where the alliance system of NATO involves ties and obligations among member nations, the connections with its Asian allies are bilateral and thus do not carry mutual obligations.

---

5. In fact, the US Navy is using Vietnamese resorts for its aircrews – one of which is only a few miles from the pond in which John McCain landed after being shot down.

Yet, despite the apparent rise in China's economic and political clout, problems exist. The current leader of the Chinese Communist Party, Xi Jinping, has embarked on a major effort to stamp out the significant corruption at the highest levels of China's political leadership, a corruption that even involved the wife of a major leader in the murder of a British businessman. Xi's problem is that to reduce corruption, he must both open up China's society and the party to the rule of law and empower China's media to report on corruption even at the highest levels of society. Xi is unlikely to take either of these crucial steps, because any form of transparency or the ability to challenge the party's positions would threaten his leadership as well as that of the party.

Xi apparently would like to see China's currency achieve the same global standing as the dollar. However, to achieve that goal the Chinese are going to have to follow the same path as a serious approach to cleaning up corruption and upholding the rule of law would involve. Without the transparency of an open society ruled by law, Xi's regime will find itself constrained by its own secrecy and authoritarian rule and remain an outsider to much of the world's financial intercourse. Any opening up of the society will in the end challenge the singular position the Chinese Communist Party enjoys, as the unchallenged and unchallengeable master of China.

China confronts a set of long-term political and economic problems that are more complex and difficult to address than those confronting Deng Xiaoping when he assumed leadership of a bankrupt Chinese state in the 1970s. The first of these is the economic impact of China's one-child policy. With a falling and aging population, as a result of smaller cohorts of the young, China may not be able to generate or amass sufficient wealth to escape the "poverty trap." It is now a near mathematical certainty that China will get old before it gets rich. With its aging population, China will soon confront problems quite similar to those Japan is facing at present. The significant difference is that the Japanese leadership must respond to electoral pressure, while the Chinese system ensures the people will have little influence.

Equally significant is that China is already confronting the sharp divide between the rich coastal areas, where much of its development has occurred, and the poverty of much of the hinterland. Since one cannot trust Chinese economic statistics, the nation's actual economic growth may well be far below what its statisticians have been reporting. The economic impact though of the current slowdown has resulted in the massive lessening of China's imports of raw materials to drive its economic expansion. Two factors exacerbate China's economic problems: the cost of Chinese labor is rising, while technological changes in the industrial sector will inevitably eliminate China's greatest competitive advantage over the past several decades, namely the masses of workers willing to work for minimal wages. China is going to find it difficult to employ not only rural workers migrating to the cities, but also those already working in the cities.

Finally, one must note that China's one-child policy has severely skewed the ratio of men to women among the country's younger population. Simply put, a substantial number of China's couples have aborted female fetuses in an effort to conceive a male child. How this will play out in terms of social dynamics is difficult to estimate. Will it make the Chinese leaders more cautious in embarking on major conflicts; or will they discover themselves under intense political pressure from the social unrest of large numbers of young men with no access to women of the same age? In some ways India will confront the same problem, but in its case the aborting of female fetuses there has largely been a matter of choice made by the upper and upper-middle classes. Thus, the impact in the Indian case might result in a further breakdown of the caste system, as young men seek out women from the lower castes—an option not open to young men in China because of the Communist Party's ruthless imposition of the one-child policy.

Perhaps the clearest indication of China's internal troubles is that its current leader, Xi Jinping, has broken with the tradition of collective rule among the leaders of the party. Instead, his current purge of corruption within the party largely appears driven by the political aim to replace those who oppose him with those who are in his camp. Moreover, he is relying on the support of the PLA's generals and admirals in this "anticorruption" campaign, a factor which goes far in explaining China's increasingly aggressive and militaristic foreign policy. While countries like the Philippines have little choice but to allow the Chinese to push them around, that is not true with the Japanese. Moreover, the Vietnamese leadership has proven itself willing to take on all comers—the French, the Americans, and the Chinese—and win whatever the cost. The dangers accompanying an incident or incidents in East Asia or Southeast Asia spiraling out of control are obvious.

China's current activities, as well as the economic and political pressures the Communist Party's leadership is already confronting, suggest that its behavior over the coming decades will be anything but constructive. It is unlikely that the Chinese will court a direct military confrontation with the United States. Nevertheless, they will continue to push at the boundaries to see how far they can intimidate their neighbors and how accommodating the United States will remain. The generally obsequious behavior of the Obama administration has only encouraged further aggressive behavior by

the Chinese. The Chinese can certainly read the geographic framework within which they find their global strategy constrained. The
island chains in the western Pacific (and it is worth underlining that
there are several chains of islands) mean that Chinese military forces
must face the fact that however the Americans choose to do it, they
are in a position to bottle China up within the confines of East Asia
and its surrounding seas.

The one caveat to that comment is the possibility that for either
political or economic reasons, the United States might abandon its
strategic responsibilities as well as its allies, turning East Asia over to
the tender mercies of the Chinese. It did follow such a path during
the interwar period, when it made no significant effort to restrain the
ruthless, aggressive war the Japanese waged on China beginning in
summer 1937. Given the current ignorance of history and the flawed
assumption of the American elites, such an abandonment of responsibility is not out of the realm of possibility.[6] Whatever its course,
China will remain a significant strategic challenge to the interest of
the United States and its allies. Above all, a successful American
strategic policy toward China is going to require knowledge of
Chinese culture, language, and politics, none of which is apparent in
abundance in America's intelligence agencies, or its universities.

INDIA AND PAKISTAN:
A RECIPE FOR CATASTROPHE?

The contrast between the historical path of India and Pakistan since
they gained independence from the British Raj in the late 1940s

---

6. For that possibility, see the discussion in Chapter 1 of this work.

underlines how extraordinarily important leadership is in the fate of states. Both states began their lives as democracies; both states possessed the great majority of their population living in abject poverty; and both confronted religious, ethnic, and social clefts running deep through their societies. India, whatever its continuing difficulties, has been a success. It has remained a democracy. It possesses a substantial number of highly educated individuals; in fact, it possesses the largest number of English speakers in the world. And it has moved energetically into the high-tech world. Admittedly, its economic success has not rivaled that of China, but part of that explanation rests on India's continued rule of law and respect for the wishes of its population. Especially noteworthy is that India's military has remained solidly outside of political controversies.

In every respect Pakistan stands in stark contrast to India's success. Its military has intervened directly in the state's politics on a number of occasions to arrest and overthrow the elected representatives of government. Pakistan's relations with India have been a disaster; its military forces have waged four major wars against India, all of which it lost. Its Inter-Services Intelligence Agency (ISI) has consistently supported radical Islamists in India, while it has been the main supporter of the Taliban both before 9/11 and then after US forces invaded and crushed Mullah Omar's regime and chased Osama bin Laden out of Afghanistan. The latter would find sanctuary within a few miles of Pakistan's military academy.

New York Times reporter Carlotta Gall has noted about the sorry story of Pakistan's leaders:

The Afghans were never advocates of terrorism, yet they bore the brunt of punishment for 9/11. Pakistan, supposedly an ally, has proven to be perfidious, driving the violence in Afghanistan for its own cynical, hegemonic reasons. Pakistan's generals and mullahs have done great harm to their people as well as their Afghan neighbors and NATO allies. Pakistan, not Afghanistan, has been the true enemy.[7]

Were the Indian-Pakistani troubles simply a matter of constant squabbling and tension between two South Asian powers, it would not matter much to long-term US interests. But both powers possess considerable numbers of nuclear weapons, and, given the disparity between Indian military and economic power on one side and Pakistani weakness on the other, there is the very real possibility that a conventional war would soon lead to a major Pakistani defeat. At that point, there is considerable likelihood that the Pakistanis would resort to nuclear weapons.

Adding to the threat of military conflict in South Asia are two factors. The first is the propensity of the ISI to support, train, and launch murderous actions by terrorists in India. The most obvious case is the November 2008 attack on various sites in and around the great Indian city of Mumbai that left 164 dead and 308 wounded. Given its track record, ISI's overly ambitious generals could well support, equip, train, and unleash the fanatics available throughout Pakistan to carry out attacks similar to what occurred in Mumbai in 2008. Such an attack on an Indian city in the future might push the Indians into the kind of retaliatory strike that could lead directly to war and an eventual exchange of nuclear weapons. The humanitarian crisis that would result in the Indian subcontinent beggars the

---

7. Carlotta Gall, *The Wrong Enemy: America in Afghanistan, 2001–2014* (Boston, 2014), p. xiv.

imagination, while the fallout and resulting ecological damage would threaten most of the rest of the globe.

That possibility is bad enough, but perhaps an equally significant threat lies in the complete collapse of the Pakistani state, as its various factions, long-inured to murderous violence, fight over the wreckage. The northwestern territory is virtually controlled by the Pakistani franchise of the Taliban, while a significant guerrilla movement is present in Baluchistan, in the country's southwestern provinces. Hopefully, the Pakistani Taliban attack in December 2014 on an army school in Peshawar, which killed 141, has awoken the army to the threat posed by the Islamic fundamentalists. But it may be too late, and the complete collapse of Pakistan is not impossible. The nightmarish question in that case would be what would happen to Pakistan's nuclear weapons? As a senior American general with extensive experience in Pakistan reported to me, the commander of the Pakistani Army had remarked that he regarded the greatest security challenge the Pakistani Army confronted was the continued security of its nuclear weapons.

IRAN AND NORTH KOREA:
THE IMPLICATION OF NUCLEAR PROLIFERATION

It is impossible to predict the path that North Korea and Iran will follow over the coming decades. Nevertheless, that said, it is clear that the international community is becoming populated by a number of states which either possess nuclear weapons or can with relatively little effort build their own nuclear weapons. The deal that the Obama administration struck with the ayatollahs of Iran supposedly to halt that nation's progress toward achieving nuclear weapons was on the face of it of doubtful utility. It certainly did nothing to reassure long-standing US allies in the Middle East, particularly Jordan and Saudi Arabia, but this administration has given little attention to America's traditional allies anywhere in the world. It may be that the Iranian hard-liners will not act until the Europeans have dismantled sanctions, when they would prove almost impossible to reimpose, before Iran continues on its path to the possession of nuclear weapons.

On the other hand, it is conceivable that the Iranians will abide by the deal and look to rebuild their military capabilities with the flood of cash that arrives at their doorstep. There are a number of factors that make Iran both interesting and unpredictable. Unlike the Arab world, which to a great extent largely consists of tribes and factions stretching from Mesopotamia to the Atlantic Ocean, the Persians possess a true nationality with a sense of its people belonging to a distinct culture and history.[8] Moreover, for all the radical changes that Khomeini introduced in the aftermath of the Shah's overthrow, he did not disparage the education of Iranian women. The result over the past three and a half decades has been the growing importance of women in Iran as an influence to mitigate the militant instincts of the ayatollahs. It also appears that the high cost of Iran's adventures in Iraq, Syria, and Lebanon will eventually affect the thinking of the senior Iranian leadership.

---

8. It does appear that this is less so the case in regard to Morocco, Algeria, and Tunisia. In the latter's case, the overthrow of the government of Tunisia at the beginning of the Arab Spring resulted in the restoration of a coherent government rather than a dissolution into tribes and terrorist groups as occurred in Libya and Syria

With regard to North Korea, there is little to say except that the continued survival of that murderous and criminal regime is surely a tribute to the ability of tyranny to survive in the face of its own extraordinary incompetence. The greatest danger of its continued nuclear program lies in the regime's possible willingness and ability to hawk its wares to those states and terrorist organizations incapable of producing nuclear weapons. However, the North Koreans are unlikely to sell such weapons to terrorists, for the same reasons that have inhibited it over the past several decades from taking on their far wealthier cousins in the south. Here the historical baggage of the past weighs on the memory of North Koreans. The events of summer 1950 underline that no matter how mealy-mouthed and strategically inept the Americans may appear, they are fully capable of altering their strategic policy in a matter of days. The result was that by the time the ferocious war ended in summer 1953, there were hardly any buildings standing in North Korea. That fact lies buried deep in the subconscious of North Korean leaders and makes them somewhat less dangerous than their behavior might suggest.

ABOUT THE AUTHOR

WILLIAMSON MURRAY GRADUATED FROM YALE UNIVERSITY IN 1963 with honors in history. He then served five years as an officer in the United States Air Force, including a tour in Southeast Asia with the 314th Tactical Airlift Wing (C-130s). He returned to Yale University where he received his PhD in military-diplomatic history, working under Hans Gatzke and Donald Kagan. He taught two years in the Yale Department of History before moving to Ohio State University in fall 1977 as a military and diplomatic historian. He received the Alumni Award for Distinguished Teaching in 1987. He took early retirement from Ohio State in 1995 as professor emeritus of history.

Dr. Murray has taught at a number of academic and military institutions, including the Air War College, the United States Military Academy, and the Naval War College. He has also served as a Secretary of the Navy Fellow at the Naval War College, the Centennial Visiting Professor at the London School of Economics, the Matthew C. Horner Professor of Military Theory at the Marine Corps University, the Charles A. Lindbergh Chair at the Smithsonian Air and Space Museum, and the Harold K. Johnson Professor of Military History at the Army War College. He served as a consultant with the Institute for Defense Analyses, where he worked on the Iraqi Perspectives Project. In 2008 he completed two years as the 1957 Distinguished Visiting Professor of naval heritage and history at the U.S. Naval Academy. From 2011 through 2013, he served as a Minerva Fellow in the Strategy and Policy Department at the Naval War College. At present he is the Ambassador Anthony D. Marshall Chair of Strategic Studies at the Marine Corps University.

He has written a wide selection of articles and books. He is the author of *The Change in the European Balance of Power, 1938–1939: The Path to Ruin* (Princeton University Press, 1984); *Luftwaffe* (Nautical & Aviation Publishing, 1985); *German Military Effectiveness* (Nautical & Aviation Publishing, 1992); *Air War in the Persian Gulf* (Nautical & Aviation Publishing, 1995); and *War in the Air, 1914–1945* (Weidenfeld & Nicholson, 1999). Professors Murray and Allan R. Millett have published an operational history of World War II, *A War to Be Won: Fighting the Second World War* (Harvard University Press, 2000), which has received rave reviews from a number of newspapers and journals, including *The Wall Street Journal, The Times Literary Supplement, The Naval War College Review, The Journal of Military History,* and *Strategic Review*. Professor Murray was a major contributor to *The Cambridge History of War*, edited by Geoffrey Parker (Cambridge University Press, 2005) and also authored with Major General Robert Scales Jr. *The Iraq War: A Military History* (Harvard University Press, 2003). He has also edited with Millett a number of books on the implications of the past for current military thinking: *Military Effectiveness*, three volumes (Allen & Unwin Book Publishers, 1988; reissued by Cambridge University Press, 2010); *Calculations: Net Assessment and the Coming of World War II* (Free Press, 1992); and *Military Innovation in the Interwar Period* (Cambridge University Press, 1996). With MacGregor Knox, Professor Murray edited *The Making of Strategy: Rulers, States, and War* (Cambridge University Press, 1994) and *The Dynamics of Military Revolution, 1300–2050* (Cambridge University Press, 2001). With

Richard Hart Sinnreich he edited *The Past as Prologue: The Importance of History to the Military Profession* (Cambridge University Press, 2006). He published *The Making of Peace: Rulers, States, and the Aftermath of War,* which he edited with Jim Lacey (Cambridge University Press, 2009), and *Conflicting Currents: Japan and the United States in the Pacific* (Praeger, 2009). In 2011 he published three books: *The Shaping of Grand Strategy: Policy, Diplomacy, and War*, which he edited with Sinnreich and Lacey (Cambridge University Press), *War, Strategy, and Military Effectiveness* (Cambridge University Press), and *Military Adaptation in War: With Fear of Change* (Cambridge University Press). In 2012 he published *Hybrid Warfare*, co-edited with Peter R. Mansoor, and in 2014 Cambridge University Press published *Successful Strategies*, co-edited with Sinnreich, and *The Iran-Iraq War*, co-authored with Kevin M. Woods. Professor Murray recently published *Grand Strategy and Military Alliances* (Cambridge University Press, 2016), co-edited with Mansoor. In September 2016 he published *A Savage War: A Military History of the Civil War*, co-authored with Wayne Wei-siang Hsieh (Princeton University Press). He has completed the manuscript for *The Battle of Generals*, co-authored with Lacey (scheduled for publication by Random House in 2017).

Some of Professor Murray's most recently published articles include: "Clausewitz Out, Computer In: Military Culture and Technological Hubris," *The National Interest*, summer 1997; "Air War in the Persian Gulf: The Limits of Air Power," *Strategic Review*, winter 1998; "Preparing to Lose the Next War?," *Strategic Review*, fall 1998; "Does Military Culture Matter?," *Orbis*, winter 1999; "The Emerging Strategic Environment: An Historian's View," *Strategic Review*, spring 1999; "Military Culture Matters," *Strategic Review*, summer

1999; "Military Experimentation in the Interwar Period," *Joint Forces Quarterly*, spring 2000; and "What History Suggests about the Future, *Orbis*, fall 2008. He has also written a number of pieces that have appeared recently in *Military History Quarterly, Military History,* and *World War II.*

INDEX

HERBERT AND JANE DWIGHT
WORKING GROUP ON
ISLAMISM AND THE
INTERNATIONAL ORDER

The Herbert and Jane Dwight Working Group on Islamism and the International Order seeks to engage in the task of reversing Islamic radicalism through reforming and strengthening the legitimate role of the state across the entire Muslim world. Efforts will draw on the intellectual resources of an array of scholars and practitioners from within the United States and abroad, to foster the pursuit of modernity, human flourishing, and the rule of law and reason in Islamic lands—developments that are critical to the very order of the international system.

Founded by Fouad Ajami, the Working Group is co-chaired by Hoover fellows Russell A. Berman and Charles Hill. Contributors to the work product of this group include Zeyno Baran, Marius Deeb, Reuel Marc Gerecht, Ziad Haider, R. John Hughes, Nibras Kazimi, Bernard Lewis, Habib C. Malik, Abbas Milani, Camille Pecastaing, Itamar Rabinovich, Colonel Joel Rayburn, Lee Smith, Samuel Tadros, and Joshua Teitelbaum.